How Little Annie Got to be the Matriarch

To Verne and Eddie
with best wishes
always —
Anne
Chanukah, 2008

How Little Annie Got to be the Matriarch

A Memoir

by

Anne E. Cohn

ISBN # 978-0-87121-050-0
0-87121-050-9

Printed in the United States of America

Dedication

I want to dedicate this memoir to those who have made me a very happy Matriarch: my beloved grandchildren, great-grandchildren and my great and grand nieces and nephews. How grateful I am that providence has granted me the good fortune to share the life and times of loved ones who are part of these new, young and vital generations.

Table of Contents

Introduction

They say "little pitchers have big ears," and I guess I was one of those little pitchers because I have vivid memories from the time I was about three years old. As I write this I am in my eighth decade. So before too much more time goes by maybe I'd better write down some of those memories for whomever is interested. A simple retelling would probably be the best way to record the story of my life and family to those who really care or are just curious. So, My Dears, here goes...........

Russian Roots

Our family was my special world. They probably weren't very special to anyone else, but my present and future family just might like to know something of its past. Papa and Mama, Jacob Euchvitz and Dora Malkin, came to the United States from Russia. They talked about "home" enough for me to get a picture of Novozybkov. And from their loving memories, it might very well have been a romanticized picture. I have never found out how long or how many generations of my family lived their lives in Novozybkov. It is now listed as among the "shtetlach" – very small towns - that no longer exist. They didn't arrive together. Papa arrived first at Ellis Island in 1906. He immigrated because a pogrom was ordered in his town, Novozybkov, Chernigov Gabernia[1] in the pale of Jewish settlement. Papa was in Manchuria at the time of that pogrom. He had traveled there on the Trans-Siberian Railroad after the Russo-Japanese War. I think he was in Harbin trying to find a better life and seek his fortune. I've read that many Russian Jews

---

[1] A province in Russia from 1802-1917 and since 1932 a province in the Ukraine known as Chernihiv Oblast.

went to Harbin either after the pogroms or after the Russian Revolution.

When Papa was six years old, his father died of pneumonia. Papa caught it as well, and for the rest of his life always suffered with a bad cough. He had two brothers and three sisters. One sister, Auntie Rosie Banks, lived in Birmingham as far back as I can remember.

Papa's widowed mother ran a little store on the grounds of the local match factory which I think belonged to someone in her family. Cousin Milton Cohen told me that Papa's brother or uncle was a well-known chemist who made the ingredients used to make matches. That was probably how my grandmother got to run her store. However, I've read that match factories were a business Jews were permitted to have in the Russian Pale of Settlement at that time.

Mama immigrated to the United States from Russia in 1907. Her maiden name was Malkin. There were seven girls in the Malkin family and one boy – Uncle Monya. I'm almost sure that Mama told me about their losing a six-year-old brother years before. Uncle Monya changed his last name to Malkove. He must have thought that Malkove sounded more Russian and less Jewish than Malkin. My Malkin grandfather was very learned and greatly respected by his family.

He also had a very beautiful singing voice and I think he must have led the prayers at Synagogue.

I don't know how this small town of Novozybkov was able to present cultural events, but they did have opera. *Faust* was one of Mama's favorites, and many years later, Mama and Papa would always make a point of attending when the Chicago Opera Company came to Birmingham. Mama was well read and was especially familiar with French literature. In the small towns of Russia, the young people's idea of socializing among their age group was to read books aloud and then discuss them.

At Mama's house, the books favoring socialism and revolution were kept hidden in the attic. But I wondered if Mama wasn't a little conservative after all. She always blamed the strict reaction to the first demands for forming the people's representatives in the government on the young revolutionaries (many Jewish) who still made fiery speeches and gloated over the new power of the "people." I think all this took place during the reign of Alexander II when the government rescinded some new rights and became more restrictive to all, especially to Jews.

I would have loved to have known some of the characters in Novozybkov. One, a natural comedian, was called Lipmanke the Meshugenah (crazy man).

Papa said Lipmanke would have been another Eddie Cantor if he had come to America.

I imagine back then the streets weren't paved, but that was probably the case here in Alabama, too, at the end of the 19th century. I thought, as they did, that it really was a very nice place to live before the pogroms. During the pogrom, Mama's family was hidden in the home of the local Russian Orthodox priest which was safely located in the church courtyard. The priest's daughter was a teacher of one of the Malkin daughters. These people were considerate enough to see that all the food served their Jewish guests was permitted by the laws of Kashrut – milk products and uncooked fruits, etc.

When I asked Mama about her father's family, she told me that her mother had once taken some of the children to Ekatarinaslav (now Dnepropetrovsk) to visit their father's family, but they received such a cold reception that she never went back. On Mama's mother's side the family name was Katz. My grandfather Katz had a thriving business and dealt in flax. His two sons manufactured rope in their own "fabrique" (factory) and were successful. Mama loved to visit her grandmother who always dressed in white on the Sabbath. There were servants and always guests.

Uncle Malkove went to work for these uncles and did very well.

Mama described the "salle" or parlor in her parents' home with lovely furniture bought in Warsaw. I'm not sure if her father ever earned much or just studied (he was revered nevertheless). Her mother did well by trading in the local market, I think. As the daughters got older, they had a stocking machine in the house and made stockings to sell. Mama went out and got the orders.

They were all educated, some self-educated, and spoke and wrote Russian as well as Yiddish. The younger ones became professionals – one a doctor, I know. Before Mama left her home for America, she enrolled her eight- year-old sister, Slava, in school. I spoke to my Aunt Slava over the phone when my husband, Marvin, and my brother, Izzy, and I were in Russia in the early 1980's. Her voice was so like Mama's that I was moved to tears. That day she told me that my mother had always been the smart one in the family. Because the Communists were still in power then and there were strict rules about travel in Russia, we didn't get to visit her in Dnepropetrovsk because it was off limits to foreigners.

My Parents Come to America

Mama traveled to the U.S. with her brother, Morris (Monya) Malkove. They embarked from Antwerp, Belgium. I'm afraid I don't know about their trip from Novozybkov to Antwerp. Uncle was married and the father of two children, Louis and Rebecca. His wife, Sonya, later packed up the family and came to Birmingham to join her husband. On his arrival in New York, Uncle Malkove, who traveled First Class, was allowed to enter the country at once. A Katz uncle, who lived in New York, met him and took him home without event. But Mama was traveling "steerage." Those immigrants in steerage had to undergo health examinations and other red tape on Ellis Island. Many years later, she told me how frightened she had been to be left alone on Ellis Island where she knew no one and didn't speak the language. The next day or maybe the one after that, she was released to her uncle who took her to his home, also.

Papa was already in the U.S. by the time Mama arrived, but he had decided to return to Russia. He told me about his job at a watch or clock company in or near New York. I think it was the Waltham Clock Company. The people working at this place, mostly immigrants, were locked in at night and their freedoms ignored. That didn't sit well with Papa. How lucky for my family that he chose to stay in America and marry Mama. They had been friends or sweethearts for a long time – maybe growing up. The story was that Papa rescued Mama when she fell into the local river. That was probably true because he was a good swimmer and used to do tricks for us when we went swimming together.

When Papa left for America he made sure that there was a dowry for his sister Rose. And she did marry an educated man. It was not long before they, too, immigrated to the U.S. and eventually settled in Birmingham. Uncle Banks was a short little man, learned, smart and with a great sense of humor. They had four sons: Isadore, Ben, Jake, and Abe. All worked hard and came up in the world financially. Sadly, now all are gone. I think every son died of cancer of some form, and I imagine we got our questionable genes from Papa's side. Papa died of pancreatic cancer at age 75.

Mama and Papa were married in Birmingham. They came south to Birmingham because neither liked New York and because Mama and Uncle Malkove had relatives here. The relatives were Rabbi Abraham and Mrs. Leibovitz. Mrs. Leibovitz was born Riva Pearl Levine, and was a blood relative of my mother. In

1907, when my parents arrived in Birmingham, Rabbi Leibovitz was a respected Rabbi at Knesseth Israel Synagogue. The three Leibovitz sons were all gifted musicians and members of well-known orchestras of the time. Their daughter, Annie Israel, was close to our family as I remember. One of her sons gained a place in the sports world as a famous announcer. His name was Mel Allen.

Papa was proud of his name, Jacob Euchvitz or Yuchvitch, and never considered changing it to one easier to pronounce or spell in America. He was an honest and honorable man with high ideals and ideas. While a young man in Novozybkov, he owned a hardware store. However, as an immigrant, married and with a growing family, he never accumulated enough money to start that kind of business here. In addition, he brought over his sister, Rose, and her family, and one of Mama's sisters, Hannah, who died during the flu epidemic of World War I. She is the one for whom I am named. Papa was always sending money home to Mama's family and his own.

Blessed with a sweet, pleasant personality and inquisitive mind, Papa enjoyed the small things in life. He was also interested in seeing what was happening around Birmingham and beyond. Mama told me that the first day he hitched up his horse and wagon to go out and peddle fruits and vegetables, she stood on the front porch and cried. However, I never thought he had any false pride.

Mama was a small woman. She had light brown hair and wore glasses always because her eyes had been injured at birth. Still, she never tired of reading. At times one might call Mama severe, but that trait was balanced by a ready and dry wit. She was a very fine home-maker and parent, and a good help mate to her husband. One couldn't call her easy-going, but she was unusually intelligent, kind and loyal. Our house was a pleasant place to bring our friends as Mama and Papa were hospitable and generous hosts in the European manner. Later, they were doting grandparents as well. As for me, I don't remember my mother being demonstrative. Even so, her love was unquestionable and deeply sincere. It seems to me that Mama had a hard time adjusting to the life and culture of the United States, even to the end of her days.

From what I can remember, Papa had an independent meat route. He sold certain kinds of meat products to the small (mostly Italian) grocery stores located in poor or black neighborhoods. He gave them credit and it all worked well until the Depression.

We had a very nice house on a large corner lot at 16th Street and 11th Avenue North. It was a one story house painted white with a porch that wrapped around to the side. There was a second entrance on the side porch. On the porch, the rocking chairs always had gleaming white cloth covers on the backs. A large window from the parlor looked out on this part of the porch. The front walk was lined with daffodils and roses which grew around the steps to the house.

Our back yard was large enough for a play area, a chicken house and a stable for Papa's horse, Tony. The stable became a garage when Tony was no longer with us. Papa always managed a small space for growing a few sunflowers. He loved the dried seeds they provided at the end of the summer. It must have reminded him of his boyhood days in Russia. There were probably servants' quarters at the house across the alley because Izzy's best playing companion was Snowball, a nice African-American boy.

The parlor was furnished with massive leather furniture with wooden parts of dark mahogany and a sofa which opened into a bed. The library table was made of the same shiny dark wood. Inside the front door, there was a small reception room furnished with wicker chairs. The dining room was nicely furnished with a walnut table, china cabinet and buffet. Some of that furniture is still in use and I noticed that it was manufactured by Tomlinson, which, even now, is considered good furniture. When I think of the dining room buffet, I remember Mama's beautiful hat that was kept in one side compartment. The hat was trimmed with lovely tan velvet roses. I don't remember her wearing that beautiful creation. Surely, it was bought for some special occasion. Maybe it was worn to Izzy's Bar Mitzvah. I just loved opening the small door and looking at Mama's hat.

The kitchen was dominated by a large wood or coal burning stove for cooking. Mama made the most delicious yeast coffee cakes, rolls and bread. On Friday, especially, our house had the wonderful aroma of cinnamon and baked goods. There was also a gas stove and a round oak dining table. Mama made her own egg noodles. I still remember the dough was stretched over a small round table to dry before being cut. Pinching off a small piece on the sly was a delight to my pallet then and even now in memory.

Funny, I don't remember meals with all the family seated together except on the enclosed back porch. That back porch also held our ice box. Oh yes, each room in the house had a fireplace. The one in the living room was especially pretty with carvings and small wooden shelves for displaying pretty things.

Later, growing up, we had wonderful mealtimes with good conversation and laughter. Heated discussions about world affairs left lasting impressions on all of us. Mama was smart and opinionated. She always preferred world affairs to talking recipes. Papa was broad minded and quiet spoken.

In Europe my parents were considered enlightened. They followed the Mitnagid movement not the Chasidic group.[2] Papa kept all holidays and had high moral standards. Money was not his top priority. I could feel their reverence and devotion to their religion and loyalty to their people. Mama created a spotless and pleasant Jewish home, kosher and traditional. Mama always lit the Shabbas candles before dark and didn't sew or do work on the Sabbath. I think of their ethical standards and remember that the children in our family respected that and tried to emulate them. Our parents cherished their beliefs. When I sat in synagogue with my parents I actually felt their reverence for G__. They didn't talk a lot about Jewish tradition, but just lived it, even though I never heard anything about a mikveh – ritual bath – and don't believe they ever followed some practices.

Mama, I think, could never get over the feelings of guilt for having left her beloved family behind to

---

[2] "Mitnagid" is the movement that opposed the Hasidic movement. The name literally means "those who oppose."

suffer while she was in this free land. She was always sending money to them until the United States broke off relations with Russia following the Communist takeover. I would be with her when she would go down to Uncle Malkove's furniture store and ask him to send their family some money too, but he was quite hard hearted and usually refused. I remember Mama crying on those occasions. In later years, I think he regretted being so unfeeling.

Papa didn't speak to Uncle Malkove for a long time. But he would drive Mama and us children over to visit the Malkoves in their really fine home on the Southside. I think I know how this came about. Papa was looking for a car to buy and found one he liked at his price at Ed Greenberg's Auto Company When Papa told Uncle Malkove about his plans, Uncle went over to Greenberg's and bought the car himself. Papa was upset at this and when next meeting Uncle, he gave his brother-in-law a good punch and knocked him down – getting at least some satisfaction.

Well, that wasn't all. Mama didn't like Papa's sister Auntie Rosie and thought her socially inferior, besides Auntie had "freckles." I'm not sure why, but at that time, "ladies" kept out of the sun and freckles were considered unladylike. I guess it was like that in Russia too. So Papa would go to visit his sister on Sunday mornings and often took me along. It seemed to me that Auntie was always cooking. After all, she had a husband and four strapping sons to feed and she also helped in their grocery store during the week. I believe she was a pretty good business woman. I was very fond of that whole family.

My Siblings: Pauline, Sarah, and Izzy

There were four children at our house: Pauline, Sarah, Izzy, and me. Pauline, the oldest, was eleven years older than I. So I remember her as a young woman. She was a lovely person. Her beautiful dark eyes were her outstanding feature. She was a gentle and sweet person, thoroughly unselfish, intelligent, and cultured. In some ways she was the typical Jewish older daughter – helping everyone in the family and contributing to the household expenses when necessary. She always had many friends who often gathered at our house and Mama always served good, home- baked refreshments.

Pauline and Sarah were just about two years apart in age and had many of the same friends and interests. Sarah was very pretty, too, with curly, chestnut hair and a ready smile. She was the tallest with long legs and good at athletics and swimming. She spoke her mind without too much worry about the effect of her words, and she prided herself on her honesty. In spite of her outspoken ways, she always had nice and loyal friends as she grew up. Her friends always respected and admired her.

After high school, Pauline went to work for Silverfield and Levine. They were jobbers in ready-to-wear. Both were very fine people and we were friends with their children. I think that they must have had reversals because, for a time, Pauline worked at Mangels, a chain dress shop. Edith Sater, Marvin's widowed aunt, worked there, too. The manager at Mangels had no pity on his employees and worked them long hours for low wages. But times were tough and these women needed their jobs.

Sarah was a pretty "tomboy." She learned to ride Izzy's bicycle before he did. Later, after just a couple of driving lessons, she filled our car with neighborhood kids and took them for a long ride to Ensley, a little town west of Birmingham. That, of course, caused a big uproar. When she took the car to school one day and brought it back with yellow paint from the streetcar, she just laughed the way she always did. According to her, the streetcar (even though on tracks) got in her way. I remember her bright smile and it seems, as I think of it, that she was usually in motion

Just like Pauline, Sarah got a job right after high school. She was a cracker jack at selling women's clothing for a little dress shop. I remember they sold two dresses for $5.75. She bought one for me and I really loved it. It was tan and brown and had a little vest. I can still see it. Usually my clothes at that stage were "hand-me-downs." When I got to be a teenager, I remember telling my sisters I wished they'd let me help pick out their clothes "because I'd be wearing them some day."

Though Izzy and I were six years apart in age, we were always very close. He grew up to be a tall and handsome man. It took a while, but his body eventually caught up with his eyes and ears. When he graduated from high school Izzy went to work in Huntsville, AL for Abe Pizitz. He lived with the Harrisons (Rose and Lou, who were originally from New York) and their three daughters. The youngest, Eleanor, became my good friend and we visited back and forth between Birmingham and Huntsville. The town clock in Huntsville's square struck on the hour. I thought that very "small town" coming from the big city of Birmingham.

Sarah was the first one in our family to get married. We first learned that she and Jake Sarasohn were "serious" when we heard that they had opened a joint savings account. They were trying to save enough money to make a trip to Palestine. Actually, Jake's parents, some of his brothers, and a sister had come to Birmingham from Palestine and they still owned property in Jerusalem. Sarah and Jake never did make it to the Jewish homeland. They were very happy together. Jake used to call her "Mrs. Darling." They had two children, Adele and Howard. During the Depression, the young couple moved in with us. Jake was a very kind person and was devoted to our family.

Sarah and Jake both died young – she at 43 and he about five years later. That was the beginning of much tragedy in our family from illness. Pauline married Sam Harris, Izzy married Estelle Eisenberg, and I became Marvin Cohn's bride. But I'll go into all that later.[3]

---

[3] At the end of these memoirs, I have attached vignettes I recently wrote about my parents and siblings.

My Early Childhood

All of us children were born at home except me! Dr. Harry Levy told me that he had brought me in his little black satchel. The satchel didn't seem very large to me, but he was the doctor and I believed him. I really did. Dr. Levy was a gentle man who took care of most of the Jewish immigrant families. I was born on July 24, 1919, Izzy's sixth birthday or the day after, (my parents thought the doctor might have written down the wrong date when Izzy was born) and they say he really didn't care for me as his birthday present. But I always loved him and he was a devoted brother in spite of the "teasing."

Both Mama and Papa were fond of Papa's niece and nephew, Rebbecah and Israel Cohen, who were married at our house after Israel returned from fighting in WWI. I was an infant at the time of the wedding, but I heard so much about it I feel like I remember it. Their sons, Milton and Wallace, were beloved cousins. Milton has left us after a long illness. Wallace is still one of my favorite people.

I remember vividly spending time at the Malkove's beautiful home on 14th Avenue South. It was a lovely home with a real ballroom on the upper floor and a call-button in each bedroom to summon servants from the kitchen. By this time, Uncle Malkove had married dear Aunt Rose and their two sons, Melvin and Bernie, had been born. They were adorable little boys. I must have been at the "maternal" age because I just loved helping take care of them and being at their house. We have remained close all through the years.

When I was about three or four-years old, I contracted scarlet fever. Since this was a very contagious disease, our house was quarantined by the Board of Health. Papa and the three other children had to move to a local Jewish woman's kosher boarding house so they could continue their usual activities. I was still sleeping in my baby bed which was a child's version of an iron bed with high sides. Mama told me that I really wasn't very sick. In fact, I somehow broke the bedroom window while recuperating.

When I was a young child, the automobile was a fairly new invention and many of our outings involved riding in the car. Some Sundays we'd go for a ride around town. We loved going through the underpass at the Terminal Railroad Station where Papa would blow the horn so we could hear the sound as it reverberated against the tunnel walls. Often the route was around Highland Avenue which, at the time, was the most posh area of Birmingham. We'd end up at Highland Ice

Cream on Avenue G. There we'd see lots of friends spending their Sunday afternoons the same way we did. There wasn't much traffic and I suppose the car was considered more of a pleasure in those days. Papa would take us for a ride on many evenings and we all enjoyed getting out and cooling off during hot evenings.

In the summer, about five or six families would get in our cars and go for picnics to St. Clair Springs, near Springville, AL. St. Clair Springs produced some kind of mineral water our immigrant elders enjoyed. The children called it "rotten egg water" because of the odor. All these folks kept kosher and so the food was prepared at home. I marvel at the work involved, but the women seemed to take it all for granted and with good cheer.

Our car was a Model T Ford, but many of our friends had big expensive cars. Of course, in those days not everyone owned a car. Besides, on almost every trip someone's auto radiator would boil over and a nice, nearby farmer would usually come to the rescue with water from his well. So it all worked out and everyone was cheerful and pleasant. I remember how afraid Mama became when we got to a part of the road with a deep embankment on one side. "Let me out. I'll walk," she'd say. After the first few times we'd tease her.

“Let us out. We’ll walk,” we cried and she and Papa would laugh with us.

I remember many Sunday outings from later years. We went to Robinwood Plunge, which was just a swimming pool with picnic grounds. Also, there was West Lake (near Bessemer) and Pine View Beach on the road to Tuscaloosa. Papa loved to see us having a good time and I guess Mama did, too. Sometimes, the Ladies Auxiliary of various Temples sold food at these picnics. It was a time that almost everyone kept kosher and the Sisterhoods worked hard and did well.

My parents had good friends and close family and enjoyed visiting with them. And the younger children were taken along. I remember as Izzy got older, he didn’t want to go visiting, but being the baby I was always included. One place Izzy and I really did enjoy was the Phillip Fishers’ in Ensley. They had a music room with a Victrola and a “Laughing Record.” Two comedians would joke around and then they would laugh and laugh which really was contagious. Izzy and I just rolled on the floor and often couldn’t stop laughing.

I must have been about three or four when Auntie Chasie Quellman (Mama’s sister) brought her two boys, Abe and Howard, to visit us in Birmingham (Heshie, the youngest, was born later). They lived in

Bronx, NY and were "city folks," When the cowherd would pass our house taking neighborhood cows up somewhere on Fountain Heights to graze, the younger boy would stand at our dining room window and get all excited, crying "moo cow, moo cow."

It wasn't long before people got rid of their cows. We never had a cow that I remember, but Arnold Royal told me that they did have a cow. They lived a few blocks away on 12th Avenue North when he was a small child. During Passover my mother would buy our milk and cheese from Mrs. Stein who kept a cow and sold her produce to her Jewish neighbors.

We did raise chickens. I'd go with Mama down to Chaimovits's Meat Market to get a chicken ritually slaughtered. For five or ten cents more, they would pluck the feathers. Needless to say, I didn't eat chicken for years. This market was on 16th Street North and 7th Avenue. On the corner the kosher deli was owned and run by the Lifshitz family.

On the other corner of 7th Avenue and 17th Street stood our shul, Knesseth Israel Synagogue. The women sat upstairs, but just a few years later separate seating was abolished. I remember sitting with Mama upstairs as a young child and with Papa downstairs.

There was a mikveh next to the shul and a Hebrew School catty-cornered. I don't remember hearing anything about the mikveh and don't think I knew anyone who used it. I really didn't know it existed. People seemed to take Jewish practices for granted then and didn't talk about it as seriously as some do now. Some things were taken for granted, but keeping kosher was never questioned by our family and friends.

Marvin grew up in a different environment on the Southside. His parents and their friends were mostly first generation Americans and they played cards and went out to eat in public restaurants. I'm sure they were kosher at home because his grandmother ran the kitchen after Ethel's family moved to Birmingham and into his family home on 15th Avenue South.

I don't know whether or not Marvin's parents enjoyed concerts and speakers as mine did, but they were card players and had many friends. Ethel and her mother both were active in the Temple Beth-El Sisterhood where Ethel was one of the first Sisterhood presidents.

In those days the YMHA was the center of Jewish cultural life. Mama and Papa went to hear the lectures. The speakers were first class. Two come to mind – Rabbi Stephen Wise and Rabbi Aba Hillel Silver. Also, Norman Thomas came to speak. He was a great orator and ran for U.S. President several times on the Socialist ticket. These men were dynamic figures. When our parents got home from these lectures and meetings we'd gather around the breakfast room table while they had coffee and discussed any new "ideas" they had heard. Of course, Zionist speakers were often world renowned.

Mama was a bit opinionated, but Papa had an open mind and gave others the right to be different. He cared very much for the downtrodden (not just in theory). And he was always a Democrat. I still remember the night we learned that Al Smith had lost the Presidency to Herbert Hoover. Papa's friends, Morris and Phillip Fisher, were probably Republicans. I was with Papa at the Morris Fishers' listening to the voting results on the radio.

I can't remember if we had gotten a radio yet. We did ultimately own a "Spartan" in a beautiful wooden cabinet and all sat around that radio and enjoyed the programs for many years. People with radios installed a lightning rod on the roofs of their houses. At that time, when radio was young, the newspapers still printed "Extras" and these newspapers were sold in neighborhoods, as well as downtown, so the news did get out pretty fast.

Some of the time frames in my memory might have gotten distorted; maybe some of the actual memories, too. But I'm trying to be honest. Izzy and I rarely remembered the past exactly the same way, which always surprised me until I realized that we each remember the past from our own perspective.

I still miss my sisters and brother. We were always close and even after marriage we remained so. We were lucky to live near each other and also near our parents. That has changed for most people now. Even my grandchildren are scattered, some in foreign countries.

Old Birmingham

Our house on 11th Avenue and 16th Street was in the heart of the Northside. This was really a Jewish section that extended from 17th Street to about 12th Street along 11th Avenue and up into the hills above called Fountain Heights. A few blocks to the south, a small neighborhood of black people occupied shotgun houses built close to the street with very little yard and quite near the railroad tracks. We often walked past this area on our way to synagogue K'nesseth Israel, which was located on the corner of 17th Street and 7th Avenue North. Also, we passed this way when walking to downtown Birmingham. The streetcar ran on 19th Street and was an easy walk if we preferred to ride to the downtown during the hot summertime.

As we passed through the black neighborhood, we often saw them having "fish fries" on the makeshift barbecue racks they had made of heavy wire. The smell was wonderful. Our wash woman, Ella, lived in this section, but in a newer house. She would pick up our clothes, wash and iron them, and bring them back to us all fresh and clean and neatly packed in a large basket. Sometimes her husband or son helped carry the basket. Mama never did have a washing machine. I don't think they were even available at the time. Our linens were sent to a commercial laundry. The laundryman picked up and delivered on certain days.

The Jewish people on the Northside were almost all immigrants from Eastern Europe. Their children, of course, were born in the U.S. A few of the parents had been born here, too. The earlier immigrants from Germany had improved their conditions by my time and, as they prospered, had moved to nicer neighborhoods on the Southside. Some of the earliest settlers in Birmingham had been Jews and they were owners of mines and big businesses.

Most of the large department stores bore Jewish names: Loveman, Joseph and Loeb, Louis Sacks, Herman Sacks, Blach's, the Ideal, Pizitz, and Burger-Phillips. Burger-Phillips sold the finest merchandise available in Birmingham and they had customers from all over the state. Of course, those were the days of the "floor walkers" who were nicely dressed and attractive men who were around to help customers find what they needed and to guide them to the elevators. Elevators were operated by attendants who called out each floor and a list of the items available on that floor. The first electric doors in the city were installed at Burger Phillips. It was called the "magic eye" door opener then. Loveman, Joseph and Loeb installed the first escalator in the city. They always had a person standing by to help their customers on to these moving stairways. All these fine institutions were located within four blocks in downtown Birmingham. This location was called "the racetrack."

Of all these stores, the only one remaining at all is The Parisian, once owned and operated by a fine old Birmingham Jewish family, but now a part of some large chain of stores located in malls. Even the name has been changed. Pizitz was a very successful business which was founded and run by Mr. Louis Pizitz who had started out in Georgia peddling with a pack on his back. He was a very fine looking tall man, dignified, with a shock of white hair as I remember. It was hard to think that he had ever been a peddler. However, many successful merchants had started out as peddlers in rural America. These beautiful old department store buildings now stand empty and forlorn – like some fine old ladies who have known much better days. No one I know goes downtown to shop and "the racetrack" is no more.

Another part of old Birmingham living only in memory now is 4th Avenue. 4th Avenue North in Birmingham runs east and west for miles. When I was growing up, "4th Avenue" meant the block on 4th between 18th and 19th Streets downtown. This area was a lively gathering place for the Jewish people in our city.

Located on both sides of the block were two or three kosher butchers, one or two delicatessens, several Italian and Greek owned grocery stores, and the Bohemian Bakery – source of delicious European breads of all sorts. (In our family, we never ate store-bought sliced bread then.) Also, there were some dry goods stores for men and a small hardware store. On the next block going west, the colored section with their own theatre and enterprises flourished. Other small businesses got their start on 4th Avenue.

On most Thursdays or Fridays Jewish women bought their Shabbat fish at these very nice Greek or Italian establishments and their meats from the kosher butchers. Mr. Chaimovitz had moved his butcher shop from the northside to the downtown location by this time. He was also a ritual slaughterer and took care of preparing the chickens, too. My Mama always traded with him. The Kaplan's and Bloomston's Kosher Butchers also did a thriving business then. Now Birmingham has no local kosher meat purveyor. Kosher meat and fowl have to be ordered from other cities or bought frozen from some of the local super markets.

Mostly, I remember Saturday evenings. Then 4th Avenue was teeming with Jewish families from all around the city. The delis were extremely busy and so was the Bohemian Bakery with its freshly baked French, rye and pumpernickel bread and rolls. During the week their bread was delivered to the homes by a family that had a regular route. I remember that during the drive home on Saturday nights we children couldn't resist the wonderful aroma of those freshly baked breads and would pinch off some to nibble on. Our parents didn't seem to mind.

The grown-ups enjoyed meeting their friends on 4th Avenue and visited while shopping. I even remember a character, rather shoddy and with a shrewd smile, who sold newspapers. Now that I think of it, he could have been a peasant who had stepped right out of a book by Tolstoy or Dostoevsky. This poor fellow loved talking Russian to the Jews from Russia. That was probably why he showed up on 4th Avenue – just to hear his native language.

Now 4th Avenue is a deserted and empty street. Most of the old buildings have been torn down. The stores are gone and so is the old Hillman Hotel (it had faced 19th Street, but had an entrance on 4th Avenue). Johnny and Sol Berman's store is gone, too. It was located on the ground floor of the Hillman Hotel.

There are some new large buildings located on 4th Avenue with parking lots. The vitality of the people who enjoyed 4th Avenue is gone along with many of the people themselves. The Jewish immigrants had brought such life, such flavor and such an interesting dimension to Birmingham. I'm afraid their children, by comparison, are pretty bland.

While we're talking about Birmingham during my early childhood, I'd like to tell you about Robert's Field, Birmingham's first airport. It was opened right before or after World War I and located in the western part of town near Ensley or Bessemer. My own memories of Robert's Field date from the 1920s. On Sundays, pilots, who were probably trained during WWI, would put on air shows. On some Sundays they sold rides on their planes to the public. The price of rides must have been reasonable. One pleasant Sunday afternoon Papa and my sister Sarah decided to take to the air. That was somewhat of a challenge and considered rather bold. Papa still had a spirit of adventure and probably wanted to experience flying freely in one of those small open planes. I remember thinking him and Sarah as very brave. Most of us today have taken airplanes to far off places and now think nothing of traveling in large jets with comfortable, pressurized cabins. But how many of us have soared through the air in a small plane with open cock-pit and the wind blowing wildly?!

Now, back to people and society I knew in those really early days in Birmingham. When I was a child, many new immigrants were doing the same thing – selling clothing and household items on the installment plan, so much down and so much a week. Their routes were around Birmingham and in the surrounding mining towns.

Some of the families on the Northside were already wealthy and successful. The scrap business was the source of most of this wealth. Unknown to them, these businessmen were pioneers in recycling. They stayed in this neighborhood because some of them had many relatives living nearby and also because the synagogue was in walking distance and they didn't ride on the Sabbath or on holidays. Finally, over time, all these families moved to other locations – many over the mountain to the newly formed areas of Mountain Brook and Forrest Park.

In those early days on 11th Avenue some of our neighbors were not Jewish. The Kirklands lived on 16th Street in a large old house. They were maiden ladies, I believe. It was because of these two women that Papa decided to spell our name "Euchvitz" instead of the more Russian "Yuchvitch." The Petersons lived across the street on 11th Avenue. Their two teenage daughters taught the neighborhood children dancing. I still remember my recital costume. It was rompers made of a green checked material. I think the dance had some theme to do with lollypops. Florine Satcher was a really cute and friendly teenager. All the Jewish boys were in love with her. She enjoyed all things Jewish and even stayed home from school on the Jewish holidays. Her family moved away so I don't know about her later life.

Our neighborhood was friendly and everyone shared a closeness not found in today's more private neighborhoods. Most of the people shared a common history and struggles. It seems to me that for us, who had lived on the Northside, it was a little like coming from a shtettel.

Birmingham was a steel town. Many people were connected to the very large steel mills operating here. Birmingham was a natural place to develop the steel industry as it is one of the few, if not only, places where the three essential products necessary for the production of steel were located – coal, iron ore and limestone. As far as I remember, no Jewish people worked as laborers in these mills. Later, some of the local young men who had engineering degrees did work there. However, when these young men learned that they were marked to never receive promotions because of their religion, they all quit one at a time. Marvin's father, Abe, and Abe's brother, Label, did own a brass foundry for a short time. I don't know what happened, but they had a falling out and never spoke again. I'm sure Uncle Label regretted his estrangement from his brother and really did try to become close to Marvin and Alan in his later years.

After his father died, Marvin became especially close to Uncle Label. Label was very religious. Marvin started saying Kaddish for his father at age 13, and growing up in Birmingham, he knew more about Judaism than his brother Alan, who grew up in Gadsden from the age of eight. Marvin and Uncle Label always seemed to have a lot in common. Uncle Label and Aunt Gussie never had any children, but I think she reared her brother's two sons. Marvin took me to visit Uncle Label and Aunt Gussie quite often. They were always very nice to me. I suppose Label was glad to see Marvin going with a "nice Jewish girl." I think Marvin's father used to take him, as a child, to visit Uncle Jacob Cohn, but I never really knew Jacob or the cousins, Harry, Nate, and Ruthi, very well.

The YMHA on the Northside, with its nice two story building, offered an indoor swimming pool, a large gymnasium, a library and an auditorium. It was a busy place with programs for both young and old. This is where I learned to swim. My sisters and brother took part in athletic programs and social affairs. Izzy and Sarah both played on the basketball teams. I had my first piano lessons there. The cost was minimal. As I became a teenager, I took an active part in the plays there directed by Benjamin Roth, the Executive Director. The YMHA was a popular venue for social club dances where young people met and often formed lasting relationships. The Jewish Federation had its offices there, too. And local Jewish clubs met in the many rooms.

Across 16th Street from our house on the corner was Jackson's Drug Store. I heard whispers then that Dr. Jackson was anti-Semitic, but I believe Dr. Jackson really was a friend who often acted as a doctor for minor ailments to help when needed. There were always people at Jackson's Drug Store. Papa's horse Tony got loose one afternoon. Mama didn't know how to handle him so she hurried over to the drug store for help. Old Smock, the handy man, came over, got hold of Tony and straightened it all out. I still remember that old, kind and gentle black man. On 11th Avenue and 13th Street was another drug store. This one was owned by Dr. Kissell. I never went there, but I think the boys in that neighborhood probably hung around Kissel's Pharmacy, also.

Birmingham had a population of around 60,000 people when I was very young. The city was very young, too, as it was incorporated only in 1871.

School Days

I started my elementary education at Martin School in Fountain Heights. My sisters and brother had attended that school before me so I felt quite at home there. I walked to school – up 16th Street and then to the school – and felt very safe most of the time. However, I had to pass one house that was a bit frightening as someone was always peeking out of the window and we children thought there was something not exactly "right" about this person (now that I think of it, it was very like the character Boo Radley in *To Kill A Mocking Bird*). I think people kept family members of that kind at home then, either because they didn't want to lose them or because they couldn't afford to institutionalize them. These people were probably not a danger to anyone, but just considered not quite normal.

Martin School was surrounded by woods on the back side. I remember clearly that one winter Izzy lost his "mackinaw"[4] while playing there. In the spring it turned up in some kind of condition. This incident

---

[4] A short, plaid, double-breasted wool coat.

caused a big hullabaloo and I guess that's why I remember it so well.

The principal, when I was at Martin, was a tall gangly man, kind of "country boy" looking and we were all scared to death of him. He had a way of keeping discipline that I don't believe would be upheld now. What he did as punishment was to make the one in question stand in the hall on one foot for some allotted time. I never heard of that anyplace else. Maybe something was done about it even then as I don't remember him being at the school very long. But then neither was I.

When I was in the second or third grade the school put on a "Tom Thumb Wedding." I was chosen to be the singer at the wedding – Madame Gali Curci, a famous opera star of those days. I must have been pretty big for my age because I wore a beautiful formal and high heels that belonged to Pauline's best friend Esther Kimerling (Meer). Esther was always very small, though.

We moved to the Southside before my 10th birthday and lived one-half block from Glen Iris School, a new building at that time and a very pleasant place. Some mornings I'd sleep until the first bell rang and still get to school on time. I had many new friends. In our neighborhood were Celia Joseph and Sara Lee

Silverfield and at Glen Iris School there were even more.

I met Blanche Marlowe Rogoff while attending Sunday School at Temple Beth-El. Beth-El was a conservative congregation. My parents joined that group and must have found it filled their needs. It was a long walk from our house to Temple Beth-El and I usually did walk if the weather permitted. Blanche, at that time, lived on 16th Street and 14th Avenue which was a few blocks closer to Temple. She was always very nice looking and slender and I remember she wore a beautiful light colored wool skirt and sweater which I admired very much. Blanche and I have continued our friendship since the age of 9 or 10 and are still close and caring now in our 80s. We both consider this a real blessing.

There were three of us in our class who stuck together at Glen Iris School. They were Adelaide Dagoff, a real beauty, and Kitty Estes of Birmingham "society" and me. Even during the depression Kitty had a chauffeur and lived in a grand house in Glen Iris Park.

Papa had our house on 11th Avenue North moved to the back of the lot, changed the entrance to 16th Street, and built two nice stores right on the front facing the avenue. One was rented by Rogers Grocery

Company, a chain from Atlanta, with a long lease. The other was rented to local people who ran what we called a creamery. Papa had great hopes for an income from these stores and also from renting out the house. Just about that time, The Great Depression of 1929 hit. I still had piano lessons and didn't feel much worry. Papa had always worked hard and we owned a big Nash car, the kind with the little flower vases by the side windows and so high on the inside that I could walk around in it. But in about a year or so, it was put up on blocks and not used any more because we couldn't afford to operate it. After that Papa would take Mama to market in his panel truck. Sometimes I'd sit in the back and was dumb enough to be embarrassed.

We lost it all in the Depression. The leases to the property on 11th Avenue were no longer worth the paper they were written on. Papa had some property in Tarrant City, and we lost that as well. I imagine we could have kept the house on 11th Avenue with the help of new homeowners' loan offered by the government if we had been occupying it. At the time, we were renting a lovely home on Virginia Avenue, and we could have bought that house for very little, but we could not afford to do so. I remember Papa walking the floor and worrying. Since he had no one to turn to, he plugged along and we always had a nice home and a nice family life, as I remember, even if we never again owned our own home and there were no tangible assets. Most people we knew were in the same financial condition, I think. I guess some of my friends' families were better off, but that didn't bother any of us.

Once, when I was about 10, Pauline had bought some really nice tan and brown shoes that tied. They had a shaped little heel. And, not so lucky for me, those shoes hurt her feet but fit me. So I had to wear them. Well, when I got to Glen Iris School wearing those shoes, there was my teacher, Miss Scott, wearing the same shoe. I knew they were for grown-ups and was so embarrassed to be wearing shoes that were obviously not bought for a little girl. But I went on and wore them out. When I wanted to join the Girl Scouts which entailed buying a uniform, I got such a tongue lashing from my Mother because of the expense that I never mentioned it again. So, of course, I couldn't march in the Armistice Day parade with the rest of the class. That's just the way things were. Times were really hard.

We had to move from our home on Virginia Avenue to one on Phelan Street (or 13th Place). The house was owned by an old Italian couple who left us a beautiful rose garden, fig trees, a peach tree and many flowers. There was a long trellis which reached from the back door of a screened porch to the back of the lot. I imagine there had been grape vines there earlier. Izzy decided to have a vegetable garden and in getting the ground ready he dug up all the dahlia bulbs and heaven knows what else. You can still see Phelan Street and that house from The Club which is located on the mountain above our old neighborhood.

There's something about The Club that for me often sparks an inexplicable and wonderful gift of memory. It's 1930 again and a ten year old little girl becomes more real than a venerable old lady. In 1930 my family resided on Phelan Street (or 13th Place South) at the foot of Red Mountain. If you look out the large glass windows of The Club, you can still see our house. It's second from the corner. There are two sets of steps leading from the sidewalk to our front porch. The whole area was hilly.

Phelan Street crossed 16th Avenue and then dead ended into Red Mountain. That's where the neighborhood children would gather to seek adventure by climbing the steep path which crossed 17th Avenue and then continued to the top of that part of the Red Mountain range.

By 1930 the iron ore mine once located there, Valley View Mine, was closed. However, a large wooden structure built out from the mine entrance remained. We could see very well how the iron ore had been transferred from the mine, moved to the end, and then dumped into the open railroad cars below. A small gauge track continued east to the wooden trestle which was built across 20th Street South and then continued on to the final destination. I've been told that this "Mineral Railroad" circled around Birmingham on its way to the western part of the area – maybe Ensley or Bessemer where the big steel companies were located. It may have been owned by L&N Railroad. Marvin lived at the foot of Red Mountain, too. He told me that on summer nights he could hear the "click, click" of the railroad from their sleeping porch.

We children had the delicious fun of doing something dangerous while feeling safe, too. The white-haired old guard at the abandoned mine was always kind to us. Sometimes a few of us would venture into the old mine. The bravest of the group reported there were bats in the dark and strange parts of the old mine. We didn't demand proof.

Some afternoons our little group would enjoy a drink of water from the well at the old farmhouse located nearby. The south side of Red mountain ran into Shades Valley. There were remnants of small company houses scattered around this lovely landscape.

I think it has all been incorporated into come kind of historical reserve now.

Many times, when attending some special dinner or posh social event at The Club now-a-days, the present fades away and in its place I see the Red Mountain of the 1930's, the old mine, and happy childhood days of innocence all very much alive.

Sarah was married in that house and I had my 16th birthday there. My sweet family planned a "surprise" party for me – but I knew about it. Izzy and Cecile Allen were supposed to be taking me to a movie that night. We left the house and some lame excuse brought us home early and I had to "act" surprised. I'm afraid that soured me on surprise parties. However, it was a nice party with lots of young boys and girls having a good time and I was introduced to some new people who were a little older than I.

Judaism

I have already told a bit about what it was like to be a young Jewish child in Birmingham, but now I'd like to explain in more detail, how we practiced our religion. From elementary school on I never attended school on Jewish holidays. We always kept Passover for the entire time and I took my matzo and hard boiled eggs to school for lunch. I never ate the hot meals offered in the school lunchrooms. If I couldn't get home for lunch, I usually ate a whole wheat raisin-bread sandwich filled with peanut butter and sliced banana. (Now I realize that was really a healthful and nourishing choice.) I attended Sunday School but not Hebrew School. Girls weren't expected to know Hebrew then. Now many females can and do read directly from the Torah. It always amazes me to see these young women, who look like lovely fashion models, take their places and read easily from the Torah

My family and my sisters were always Zionists. Mama and Papa remembered buying Shekels to be used for settling Jews in Palestine even as young people in Russia. Papa's fondest wish was to be able to give more to the United Palestine Appeal. Pauline and Sarah were very active members of Junior Hadassah and

Pauline, especially, reached a high office in the Southern District of Junior Hadassah. It makes me sad to realize that neither one ever got to visit the State of Israel.

My sisters always had many friends. They were active young Zionists and leaders in Junior Hadassah and other groups. Sarah led Young Judea clubs for the younger girls. Mama, always a warm and hospitable hostess, greeted our friends and served refreshments every week. Her spice cakes and marble cakes were favorites. Knowing my family's devotion to the Jewish homeland, Rabbi Bengis gave me that subject to speak on at my Confirmation at Temple Beth-El. I have surely been blessed to have visited Israel about six times with Marvin and twice since he left us.

As a young child, I'd play outside the Shule with the other children because the services were so long and we weren't expected to sit quietly for hours. I remember Papa always coming to get me when the Shofar was about to be sounded. I thought until recently that he just wanted me to enjoy hearing that ancient and soul-touching sound just for the pleasure of it. It wasn't until Rosh Hashanah 2002 that I read in the prayer book that every Jew must hear the Shofar on Rosh Hashanah. Papa probably knew about that law. He usually had good reasons for what he did.

During these young days, and later too, being Jewish was a natural and comfortable position for me. I knew where I belonged and so did my family. We felt that we were "different" from most of the population. But "different" never meant "inferior." If we were poorer, it simply didn't matter as far as our real worth was concerned. Our way of life was accepted by us without reservation. I'd never heard of the German-Jewish/Reform Jews at that time so their superiority was lost on me.

My parents must have realized that their children understood some Yiddish because they spoke Russian when the conversation was not for our ears. I didn't even know I could speak Yiddish until Marvin and I made our first trip to Israel in 1968. At that time we were visiting a Malben, which is a home for the aged. There I saw old women who had already experienced much tragedy in Europe and were now left without any family. My heart went out to these old ladies and I began to speak to them in Yiddish. Even though most Israelis preferred Hebrew and looked down on Yiddish, these old folks were happy to converse with a stranger who seemed to care about them. Only later did I realize that I had used the familiar form of speech in addressing them. Of course that was all I had heard at home among the family and didn't know any better. Still I don't think these ladies were insulted by my “familiarity.” They were wise enough to understand from my poor Yiddish that I was a neophyte but with good intentions.

Although I had been born into an Orthodox Jewish family and educated to confirmation at a Conservative Temple, it was not until years later, at a Reform Temple after my marriage, that Marvin and I both developed our love of and fierce loyalty to Judaism and the Jewish people. Our years of full participation in all aspects of Jewish life in Gadsden, and to some extent in the greater Jewish world, greatly influenced our maturity and philosophy of life. For me personally, I realize now that our Temple and its Sisterhood were really my "university."

My future husband Marvin Cohn

Marvin came into my life when I was about 14. Perry Schwartz brought him over to see me one evening. At that age no one drove a car and we lived in walking distance of each other. I lived on 13th Place and they lived between 16th and 17th Streets. Marvin's father, Abe Cohn, had died at age 42 when Marvin was about 13. He became a Bar Mitzvah and a "Kadishel" the same year as he prayed Kadish for his young father at Temple Beth-El. The men at the minyan everyday became his mentors. In his later years he remembered and was grateful to them for helping him develop his strong bond with the Jewish people and Judaism.

Marvin's whole family lived in a very nice two-story brick home, but Ethel had to give it up during the Great Depression. Abe was a very smart and energetic business man, successful until the Depression wiped him out. I believe he would have made a come-back if he had lived. As it turned out, he left his beautiful 33 year-old wife and two sons, ages 14 and 8, with little financial security. Ethel knew nothing about the financial world and had never used a checking account. She showed much courage and strength when she moved her family to Gadsden. She learned how to run the scrap business, took care of herself and her children, and made the best of her life. She never became hardened or embittered at her lot. She was a practical person and didn't try to shield the children from life's realities. The Jewish people in the Gadsden community were very kind and friendly to her. The children helped her as much as they were able and learned about business at a very young age.

This might be a good place to tell something of Ethel's family. Marvin's great grandfather, Louis Lipsitz, emigrated from Lithuania to South Carolina with his three sons, a daughter and his wife, who died early on. Grandpa (Reuben was Papa) was remembered as a crotchety old man who used to send Marvin to the drug store regularly to buy his "cough" medicine which had a high percentage of alcohol. This was during Prohibition when it was against the law to buy or sell liquor. Grandpa had his own remedies for everything.

Once, Edith took Grandpa to see Dr. Harry Shugerman about headaches. When Grandpa removed his derby hat, the doctor found his head covered with mashed sweet potatoes. (I've heard that sweet potatoes are good for us, but never knew they could be absorbed from the outside. Still, they could contain some healing element. I suppose.)

Papa Reuben had a brother and a sister in South Carolina and they were well respected and loved. Uncle Phil, another brother, was much younger. He was educated in the U.S. and became a very successful jeweler in Fairmont, WV. They had other family in small towns in South Carolina, especially in Beaufort and in Savannah, Georgia. These folks ran small country stores, struggled at first and then were successful.

Papa Reuben and Mama Lena were distant (I don't know how distant) cousins so they shared lots of family. I'd always heard Lena express pride in her brothers in Lithuania. She had visited back there in about 1925. These brothers were *Photographers to the Czar*. Sometimes that was taken with a little grain of salt. When Marvin and I were in Israel around 1968, we found out it was true. Marvin and I had invited Ethel's cousin, Lila Jasvoin Titova, and her daughter Irina, to stay at our hotel with us in Tel Aviv. We introduced Lila to some of our traveling companions and they enjoyed a lively conversation in Russian. Even Marvin and I could understand it when the word "photographer" with a Russian accent was spoken. Actually, this man had known Lila's father and uncle in Kounes, Lithuania. The pictures we had seen of Lena's brother showed a handsome and debonair man, well dressed and, in fact, wearing boots and a riding habit. Now Lila has traced her family on the Internet and found the Jasvoins were truly photographers to the last Czar. Their pictures of the Russian Royal Family are readily available.

Ethel's family moved from Savannah to Birmingham and they all lived with the Cohns – Ethel, Abe and their two children. Abe was very good to all of his wife's family. Edith came back to Birmingham with her two sons, Joel and Rex when she was widowed. Ethel's younger sisters, Frieda and Rose, were married in a few years. Her mother, Lena Lipsitz, ran the household as the matriarch and was greatly honored and respected. She ran the kitchen with "Mammy," the black helper. Eddie was the oldest and a World War I veteran. He was a member of the famous Rainbow Division from Alabama. Rose eloped with Bob Jacobs who was from an old German family that was well established and respected. Sadly, that marriage ended in divorce because of Bob's obsession with gambling. This union brought two lovely children to the family group – Robert and Harriet. Frieda had married Jack Cowan, an Irish Jew and a true gentleman. They never had children, but reared Harriet with much love and devotion.

Then there was "Yank" (Jerome Lipsitz) who was somewhat of a loner, but devoted to his Mother and family. Max, the youngest, was small but very handsome and charming. He married Esther Turner from Ensley (Corolla beauty when at the University of Alabama) and they produced Michael and Lynne Robin.

I almost forgot Ethel's father, Reuben, and no wonder with all the strong female characters in the family. The fact that he was never successful in business and couldn't contribute much to the financial welfare of the family made him rather invisible. Lena had become the strong head of the family. But Reuben did help Ethel get started in the scrap business that was left to her when Abe died. He didn't seem to mind living in Gadsden. In fact, he was with us in Gadsden when Marvin and I were getting ready to open the first Marvin's store. He and I were repainting the old shelves and I made sure that he was dressed warmly as the weather had turned cold. I did notice that Papa Reuben would go out to the car to rest quite often, but I didn't realize that he was feeling ill until he had returned to Birmingham and ended up in the hospital. He passed away a short few months later. He had spent a lot of time with Marvin and me after we were married and I liked him very much. Our son, Robert, is named for him.

High School

By the time we got to Ramsay High, the Marlowe's had moved to the other side of 20th Street to 42nd Street South. Blanche and I spent many nights together – thinking nothing of sharing a twin bed at both our houses.

Once in high school, Kitty planned to join a sorority and she told me she was getting a fur coat. Well, Jewish girls weren't considered sorority material. Adelaide who was half-Jewish was probably just too poor. After our years in grade school together, we began to drift apart.

Eventually, I was invited to join a Jewish sorority. Some of my best friends were also asked to join and to attend their annual banquet and dance. I wore a long ice blue dress. Of course, I wore the same clothes over and over again. But one summer I did get a new cotton print long summer formal. When I wore it to the next dance, one of the boys told me he didn't know who I was in that new dress. It was pretty. Oh, well.

My group wasn't interested in continuing this sorority, so when the older girls graduated, it fell apart. During the summer before high school, Adelaide and I spent a delicious afternoon on our front steps on Phelan Street (she lived across the street) making up outlandish and wonderful lies about all the plans we had for our social life at Ramsay High. Of course, we were going to tell Kitty all this, but our "trio" never met again.

When I was about 15, Jake Sarasohn gave me driving lessons. Cars had gear shifts then so I needed practice starting and stopping (as much as Papa doted on me, he didn't have the patience to teach me to drive). About this time, when I was still learning to drive, Mama needed to go to 4th Avenue North from our house on 13th Place South. I think she wanted to buy fish for Shabbat. She asked me to drive her. I was scared to death and prayed all the way that I wouldn't have to park parallel. I didn't. We got there and back safely with whatever it was Mama had to get and I've been driving ever since. Driver's licenses weren't required back then and, as you can imagine, traffic was not nearly as heavy as it is now. I think I learned to drive on a Model-A Ford.

Driving notwithstanding, High School wasn't a carefree and glamorous time for me. I did very well in my studies and was active in some of the extracurricular activities. I always took five major subjects instead of the four required so I could get in some commercial courses like typing, shorthand and bookkeeping because I knew I'd have to get a job and go to work after graduation

Socially, I had a good time and was invited to many dances and parties in the Jewish community. I dated and was invited to the Jewish club dances at the YMHA and at the Pickwick Club and local hotels, as well as to the fraternity affairs held in Birmingham mostly by Kappa Nu alumnae. A big AZA convention for Southern chapters was held in Birmingham one winter and it was a chance to meet lots of people from other cities and have a great time. I even got a new evening gown. It was long and red – a beauty.

In high school there was a definite division between Jews and non-Jews. I knew very well where I belonged. I knew especially that I was an outsider to the Birmingham "society" crowd – many of whom were driven to school every morning by the family chauffeur. Later, as the depression got worse, family members did the driving. Still, I was elected president of the French Club, a contributor to the school newspaper and also, a member of the National Honor Society. There was surely anti-Semitism, but it was buried under good manners.

Marvin had moved to Gadsden, but came back to Birmingham for about a year and stayed with grandparents and all the rest of the Lipsitz clan. They had lost the beautiful home on 15th Avenue by then and lived in a smaller place while he attended Ramsay. He was always big for his age and would often borrow Max's Buick roadster and take friends for a ride in the rumble seat (it opened from the back of the car – near the trunk). He once took a corner too short and broke the wooden spokes on one of the wheels. And he really caught it, but Max still let him drive.

My graduation day wasn't a happy one for me. I knew that I was expected to go to work and I was not properly prepared to get a job. However, I do remember my family trying to make it special and giving me a beautiful bouquet of flowers after the program. (We didn't have an auditorium at Ramsay so the event was held at Phillips High School.) I loved them for their kindness and caring. I wasn't yet 17 as my 17th birthday was to be on July 24, 1936.

I think many in the National Honor Society were offered scholarships to the University of Iowa. I was, also, but I never even considered going as it was too far away. I didn't know about getting counseling at school and no one offered help. During that summer I did get in the car and drive out to Birmingham Southern College. There I talked to the bursar – Mr. Yeilding. He was very nice to me and told me they could give me my tuition, but I would have to furnish my own books.

It didn't occur to me to talk to him about doing some work at the college to earn enough for books. Then too, there was the question of getting from my house to the campus every day. (Recently, Arnold told me about his experience in attending Southern. He rode the street car, getting a transfer and it probably took some time. The streetcar fare then was seven cents and the transfer cost two cents more. I believe there were books of carfare available which cost less.)

That night, when I told the family all this, they didn't encourage me. Pauline advised that it would be better for me to go to work, earn enough for some nice clothes and get a good husband. I certainly did get a wonderful husband and blessed life. Even so, there has always been a little bit of regret nagging on the edges.

Living in a household where learning was respected and reading a large part of life, it seems strange that I got such advice and followed it. But on the other hand, I lived in a household where ideas were important and I remember to this day some of the books my sisters were always reading and I read them, too. Just now some of these same writers are being discussed in my Sunday study group. All this was so long ago. I'm now in my 84th year. Life before my marriage seems so short a time and almost pressed together in a small space. I can't seem to put it all in consecutive order. So I guess I'll have to add things as they come to me. My dear friend, Janice Lowi (now no longer with us) once told me that I had a mind like popcorn and you know how that can get out of control.

Young Adulthood

I still remember the summer after my high school graduation. I didn't know how to go about getting a job and wasn't really equipped to hold one. At Ramsay I had gotten some knowledge of commercial courses, but really hadn't taken them seriously enough. I still have dreams about trying to type an important letter and starting it over and over again and never getting it right – so frustrating.

Finally, Pauline got me a job at Silverfield and Levine Jobbing Company where she worked as head bookkeeper. I helped in the office and also waited on the trade. At that time, peddlers brought in their customers to select dresses or coats which were bought on the installment plan – nothing much down and so much a week. The bosses were very nice to me and my salary was $8.00 per week. I probably wasn't worth any more. I did learn how to post on the booking machine and had a wonderful time trying on the new styles as they arrived for stock.

While I was at Silverfield and Levine, Mr. and Mrs. Levine and their star salesman, Steve Colpack, were planning to drive to New York on a buying trip. They were connected with a New York buying office. I still don't know how it came about but they took me on this trip. We stayed at tourist homes. During the Depression some people rented out rooms in their houses to tourists if they were lucky enough to reside on a well traveled route. At that time the highways ran through all the towns on the way – right through the main streets. I didn't have much money but tried to pay for my own meals. They paid for the lodging as I couldn't afford that, too. I shared a room with Mrs. Levine and I guess Mr. Levine bunked with Steve Colpack. When we got to New York City, they registered at the Lincoln Hotel located right across the street from Grand Central Station. The company's New York buyer took us all out to dinner at a fine hotel that first night. The next day I moved out and went to stay with my relatives, the Quellmans, who lived in the Bronx. Auntie Chashie Quellman was Mama's sister. She and her family were welcoming and gracious – especially Howard who was just a bit older than I. He took me dancing at the famous Roseland Dance Hall and we had a good time together. Roseland was one of those places a single man could buy tickets for dancing with the girls who worked there. Two orchestras took turns playing and couples came there to dance, too. It was really quite respectable.

While I was in New York a boy I knew in Birmingham (originally from New York) came to town and took me out and showed me some of New York City. Our stay was probably not even a whole week. The morning I was to meet the Levine's at the Lincoln Hotel for departure, none of the Quellman family were available to take me to Manhattan. The youngest boy, Heshie, walked me to the subway stop on his way to school. I had instructions about when to get off the subway. My station was right under the Lincoln Hotel. I sat glued to the window, watching the numbers flash by as the train made its way to my destination. Finally, the right number showed up and I got off the train. As I walked along to the hotel, my suitcase got a little heavy and I found myself stopping and putting it down for a short rest. During one of those "rests," a very nice looking, well dressed black man approached me and offered to carry my bag. What a relief. He escorted me with my bag right to the Lincoln Hotel lobby. I knew instinctively not to insult this gentleman by offering him any kind of gratuity but I was really overwhelmed (coming from the Deep South at that time in about 1938 or so) and knew this was quite an extraordinary occurrence. So I just thanked him sincerely and that was that. My traveling companions who were meeting me in the lobby didn't say a word. I seem to remember that incident better than any other on the trip.

With my meager salary at Silverfield and Levine, I was paying my dentist, Chink (Dr. Leon) Weinstein, each week for some work that was quite expensive and even managed to take out an insurance policy for $1,000. This was like a savings plan, but I can't remember the proper name for that kind of policy. Of course, I lived at home and had no expenses and I got all my clothing – including hose and underclothes wholesale. Later, I did contribute a minimal amount to the house expenses.

Though high school graduation had not been a glorious time for me, I had to face the future and go to work. My time at Silverfield and Levine was a period of growth, but I never did get a raise. Their accountant (Mr. Michaels) offered me a job at Guarantee Shoe Company in downtown Birmingham as a bookkeeper-stenographer and the salary was to be $25 per week.

By now I had learned how to use a bookkeeping machine so could do the posting of charge accounts, figure discounts, make out the checks and also do the payroll–not so complicated as now. As for the other duties, I just followed what was already in place. At times I did the letter writing and in a pinch had to act as wrapper and cashier. Eventually, I got an assistant and that was a big help.

The bosses were Mr. Sol Shugerman and Mr. J. Goldstein. Mr. Shugerman was tall and heavy with a nice personality and a ready smile. Mr. Goldstein was old and small and thin. He would get to the store around 10 AM. On his arrival everyone was tense – even Mr. Shugerman. His driver was a young black man who lived in the alley behind Mr. Goldstein's house and grew up in the neighborhood with Marvin, as the Goldstein's lived across the street on 15th Avenue South. He would sometimes talk to me about his poor prospects in comparison with the white boys he played with as a child.

After working at the shoe store for two years, I informed the manager that I was leaving to get married. He tried to discourage me saying, "You can do much better." He was older, but not wiser – for sure.

Marvin and Anne

Marvin decided to attend Georgia Military Academy near Atlanta for his high school senior year, but he quit high school a month before graduation. On learning this, I begged him to stay on. There may have been money problems about the tuition involved. At that time, he could have used a strong person to guide him. I often wondered what he would have become with the advantages and broadening influences of a college education. Marvin was very bright and wise and he had the gift of vision. More than that, he had a compassionate soul and a good and noble heart. He developed into a superior person, respected and admired and loved by even his casual friends and cherished by those who really knew him well.

There were times when we didn't see each other for quite a while. Marvin was in Gadsden and I lived in Birmingham. Somehow we managed to spend almost every New Year's Eve together from the time we were teens until we could no longer be together at all. There were two New Years rituals for us. After attending some party or dance with friends, just the two of us would drive over to a park on Highland Avenue and Marvin would shoot a Roman candle into the dark sky.

Then we'd drive over to Baker Dairy, park in front of their big window and watch the cows being milked by new modern machinery. I never thought about it then, but the Roman candle shooting high into the sky somehow expressed our joy of life and hope for the future. The prosaic milking of the Baker's cows, on the other hand, brought us pleasure from mundane every day things just as long as we were together. By this hour it was close to dawn. The New Year had been welcomed with spirit and now was well on its way, so we could go home to restful sleep.

By now Marvin was coming to Birmingham pretty often. He could find more "business" in Birmingham. Papa once smiled and told us that it was because of Marvin that the state of Alabama was building a new highway between Birmingham and Gadsden. The long distance operator knew all about our romance and sometimes gave Marvin unsolicited advice. I didn't go "steady" until we were engaged so I dated some other boys, too. One of them bought a series of tickets for horseback riding and took me riding every Sunday.

The stables must have been in the vicinity of what is now part of Mountain Brook and the bridle paths took us near the present day Mountain Brook Club. One Sunday Marvin paid me a surprise visit and

I already had plans to go riding with this other fellow. When I explained that I couldn't break the date because the other boy had spent so much money for the tickets, Marvin hit the ceiling. After some strong language, he told me he'd buy the blank, blank tickets.

I went on and "did the right thing." When it came time for me to tell this fellow I was getting married to Marvin, he cried. I'm glad I wasn't a heart breaker because that was pretty awful.

I have often wondered how a young and inexperienced girl knows that a certain boy has the character and attributes to become the kind of man she will admire and with whom she wants to spend her life. When Marvin and I got to the point that we were very unhappy apart – we decided to marry and go on together.

Even though Pauline was not yet married, neither she nor the family expressed concern that the younger sister (by 11 years) was marrying first. Pauline was as supportive and as loving as ever. And Marvin's mother, Ethel, accepted the plan which was for me to move into her house in Gadsden as part of her family. It never occurred to me to object to this arrangement. That was the only way it could come about.

One day Ethel came to my office at Guarantee Shoes to take me to lunch. While we were together, she wanted to take me to select my wedding ring. Her brothers Max and Yank had a Pawn Shop by this time and sold jewelry. That day a jewelry salesman was to call on them. She showed me a lovely ring with small diamonds set all around it. I thought it too expensive and told her I didn't need one so expensive. But they were getting it wholesale and that helped. I was really quite thrilled and excited. My engagement ring came from Uncle Phil Lipson (Reuben's brother) who was a successful jeweler in Fairmont, West Virginia. The family always got their valuable jewelry wholesale from Uncle Phil.

Marvin and I were married in August of 1940 at my parents' home on 14th Avenue South near Glen Iris School. The ceremony took place before the fireplace in the large living room. I just wanted a reception with light refreshments, but Papa wanted a meal so the Shiva Broches could be recited. Now I've noticed they recite these prayers as part of the wedding ceremony. The bride walks around the groom seven times or as many times as they plan. At that time I had never heard of this custom. Even though the expense was a hardship, we had a meal and the prayers were recited at the meal. We couldn't afford a traditional wedding cake then, but finally got a beautiful one on celebrating our 25th wedding anniversary at The Club – no less.

My going away outfit consisted of a cotton shirt-waist dress, saddle oxfords and bobby sox. We drove off to New Orleans as happy as anyone could be and spent several days at the Roosevelt Hotel. We had a great time and bought our first household object, the lovely porcelain lady which remains in our breakfront today. She cost about $6.00 at an antique shop in the French Quarter and wasn't very valuable then and probably isn't now, but I fell in love with her and Marvin bought her for me. Maybe by this time, 68 years later, her value has increased.

When Marvin had to wire home for more money, I was mortified. Ethel came through for us and off we drove to Biloxi. On Ship Island I got terribly sunburned even though we stayed covered with an umbrella and robes. When we got back to Gadsden, I could only wear a bandana-like top with shoulders and arms uncovered.

I remained attached to my own family in Birmingham. Two months after my wedding, when my sister Sarah was about to deliver Howard, I went to Birmingham to help Mama take care of Adele. (I don't know why we always thought Mama was "old" and needed help. She was 58 at this time.) The baby was delivered and I stayed a few extra days, not realizing that Marvin was feeling very neglected at home.

He phoned to complain and my family quite agreed with him. Izzy drove me home to Gadsden that night. When we got there, Marvin wasn't even home but at the Princess Theatre. Izzy took me right down there and left me with my husband. I guess I finally understood that my place was with him even though I stayed devoted to my family and he joined me in that devotion all our life together.

At first, Ethel, Alan, Marvin, and I lived in a duplex on Haralson Avenue. Ethel went to work everyday and left me in charge of the house. They already had a cook who came in everyday, did housework and prepared a large noon meal. At that time almost everyone came home for dinner at noon and had a lighter meal at night. Gadsden was a small town and it didn't take long to get home. We soon found a much nicer and larger duplex at 944 Chestnut Street. It was very spacious. Three bedrooms upstairs, one quite large with a fireplace, a living room, dining room, breakfast room, kitchen, and back porch downstairs. There was also a basement with a coal furnace. The bathroom was upstairs. Old Dr. Guice was our landlord. He owned a lot of real estate, especially rental homes. Since our rent was frozen at $40.00 per month, he refused to spend any money on upkeep. Our rent was so cheap we didn't mind keeping up the property ourselves. When the children came along, we added a large gate to the front porch. It was a convenient location with nice neighbors and we ended up living there for 10 years.

I was welcomed by the Jewish families of Gadsden, especially Janice Lowi and Edna and Vera Lowi. Gussie Garry wasn't much older than I, but she already had two children. Bertha Berman and her sister, Anne Philipson, were good friends. Also, there were Rose and Harry Greenberg, originally from Birmingham, who had known me as a small child. Janice Lowi became a dear friend and someone to admire and try to emulate.

Some of our neighbors were Jewish, too. Ida and Abe Shugarman and their daughter Jeanne lived on the corner. My father and Abe's father had been friends for many years and Ida was a Nichols from Birmingham. They had known my family and me as a child and were wonderful to us. I even borrowed Ida's vacuum cleaner once in a while. They were really good to us. I remember we had Seder with them the year Alfred was born. In fact, the day he was born I thought I was having a stomach ache from too much matzo!

There weren't any young Jewish couples except for the Harry Allens. They had grown up in Gadsden and had a circle of friends. We were included and invited to join them. I was accustomed to going with Jewish people and felt happier in their company. During the day all age groups of women mixed. The ladies were really good and kind to me. Ethel and Marvin were well liked and that didn't hurt.

Once Mama came up to visit and I took her to our weekly "sewing club." When she got home she told the family about it and about one of the "girls" who was 72 years old. That was Aunt Rosie, Mrs. Rosenbaum who, with her husband, celebrated their 50th wedding anniversary that year with a large party given by her daughter from New York. (I was 21.)

The one girl my age was Faye Stamm, Janice Lowi's cousin, who had been reared by Janice's mother and her aunt. Faye's mother had died very young and left Faye and her brother. Faye's father had died by the time I got to Gadsden, but he had been an owner of Hagedorn's Department Store. In a year or so Faye married and moved to her husband's home in Montgomery.

The Hagedorns, with a whole group, had moved to Gadsden from Philadelphia, PA to operate the commissary at the Dwight Cotton Mills in Alabama City. Gadsden did have an educated and cultured group of interesting people. For entertainment there were card games every night. Ethel played with all the groups. She'd come home from the scrap yard, bathe and dress for the evening. In summer she wore a white pique dress and a pretty blue pin. She'd look immaculate and beautiful and out she'd go and usually was a winner at poker.

After Marvin and I had been married a little over a year, Ethel married Sam Green, a widower from Middletown, NY. They were introduced by the Kahns of Gadsden who had once had a mill in Norwich, NY, and knew Sam's sister and brother-in-law, the Selkowitzs. When Ethel moved to Middletown Alan elected to stay in Gadsden with us. He went off to Columbia Military Academy in Columbia, TN and graduated there, but his home was always with us. He brought his friends over often and they stayed for meals many times. All of Marvin's family came and went during the summers. However, I'm getting ahead of myself.

Those first years in Gadsden seem so long ago and memories are darting in and out. After Ethel married Sam Green and moved away, I would go out to the Atlas Iron and Metal Company, a scrap yard then occupying a full square block on Forrest Avenue, and help out when needed. We had a bookkeeper named Inez Mitchell who had worked for Ethel for a number of years, but in a pinch I'd come out and help. I learned to weigh trucks and keep records, but never learned how to buy scrap iron and what to pay. In addition to iron, the scrap yard dealt in brass, copper, and other metals.

World War II

I remember Sunday, December 7, 1941 and Pearl Harbor. We had invited a distant cousin of Ethel's, Willie Berkowitz from Liberty, NY and a couple of his friends over for Sunday dinner. These men were stationed at Fort McClelland as part of a group of New Yorkers called up to serve with their state National Guard units. On that day, we had finished dinner and were all visiting in the living room. The radio was turned onto the Sunday Symphony Concert. Suddenly, the music stopped and an announcement came on telling us about Pearl Harbor. President Roosevelt made his famous speech about "a day that will live in infamy." This was followed by instructions for all men stationed at Fort McClelland to return to their post at once. Willie and his friends left our house immediately for Anniston and we never saw them again. I'm almost sure that Willie returned home safely after the war as Ethel was in touch with his family who lived near her new home in Middletown, NY.

Those days in Gadsden seem so long ago, even farther away than my childhood. I wonder why. When Camp Sibert opened in Attalla we had a nice group of young couples to socialize with. Most of the men were Second Lieutenants, just out of college. There were lots of Jewish couples mostly from northern states. We remained friends with some all through the years especially Tillie and Joe Zallen from Boston.

Two of our other good "Northern" friends were Tony and Bubbles Vinocur from Cleveland, OH. Marvin saw them when he made several trips to Cleveland after the war, but I never did. Writing this so many years later makes me wonder whether they remember it all and if they think of us. After all I'm 85 and Marvin is gone. Many of them probably aren't still alive. I know Tillie Zallen died a few years ago in Ft. Lauderdale where they had moved because of her poor health. We attended Tillie's and Joe's older daughter's wedding in Boston. Also, when my Linda Gail was in school in Boston we had occasion to see them and in Ft.Lauderdale, too. The Zallens brought their three children and came to visit us right after we had moved into our house on Fairoaks.

Continuing more about the war years, Camp Sibert was a temporary camp for chemical training. At first, there was only a "tent city" and muddy roads. When we'd go to a movie on Broad Street in Gadsden, there would be many service men attending and most would be coughing – probably because of the bad conditions of the camp that first winter. Later, the roads were paved and nice barracks were built. Apartments and houses were scarce, and many local people rented out rooms to soldiers stationed at Camp Sibert. Sibert remained a temporary camp and was dismantled after World War II. As Dickens wrote in *A Tale of Two Cities*, this too, "was the best of times and the worst of times." Many of our friends were shipped overseas from Sibert and their wives returned to their homes to wait out the war.

The scrap business was considered a war industry, but as the U.S. got more and more into the conflagration the draft was invoked and many older and married men were drafted. So Marvin was finally called up. He didn't tell me about it and I was in Birmingham at Mama and Papa's apartment when he came in to tell me he had been designated "4 F." I think he always felt bad about that. However, he did have a family to support. Alfred was born April 7, 1942 and God knows I was happy to have my husband at home. During the war, workers were supposed to be frozen in jobs which were connected to the war effort. Marvin never stopped any of his men from getting better jobs at Republic Steel in Gadsden. The equipment, shears, presses, the trucks and so forth were a big investment. We always made a living, but Marvin didn't really like that business. However, he knew how to bid on merchandise and had some good friends at several of the big companies around. I don't remember exactly why he decided to give up Atlas Iron and Metal Company, but I never heard him express any regret about that decision. In the interim, between the scrap business and the opening of Marvin's, he bid on a lot of merchandise being sold by the U.S. Army. At one point, he'd bought a very large number of GI water proof raincoats and sold them from an unoccupied store downtown.

One of our neighbors was the Herndon family. Dan Herndon was an executive at Republic Steel. There were three girls and one boy in his family and we were very close to all. Dan, the son, had a wonderful time helping on the "raincoat deal." When our children came along the Herndon kids would play "Hanukkah Man" and leave our children's gifts on the front porch for us every night. Marie Herndon, their mother, had been a nurse and was a great help to me when my children were ill. They were devout Catholics.

On the other side lived the Dolans, another Catholic family with Republic Steel. They were older and such lovely people. Mrs. Margaret Dolan was a large woman, good and kind and Uncle Pete Dolan was a great fellow. Alfred, especially, spent a lot of time with "Uncle Pete" who taught him how to grease his tricycle and fix things. They had an old Brindle Bulldog named Micky. During the war when help was hard to keep, Micky would notice that there was a new nursemaid with the children and would always accompany them on their walks around the neighborhood. Miss Katherine was Margaret Dolan's sister. She had suffered a stroke and spent much time on their screened front porch. She probably enjoyed Alfred and Linda's visits – they were good company. These good people never had children of their own, but raised a whole family of orphaned nieces and nephews. They even kept a grandniece during this time. They were such good and fine friends.

It always worked out that we didn't have any help during the High Holy days. Mrs. Dolan kept the children several times so I could go to Temple. On Easter she always had Easter baskets for our children, never bringing up any religious issue. When Pete retired they moved back to Joliet, IL. On one of our trips to Chicago for the Hardware Show, Marvin and I took a train and went to Joliet to see them. Margaret's mind had deteriorated by then and I didn't think she really knew us, but Pete was a prince as always.

Everyone had to make sacrifices to help the war effort. We did all the things civilians could do – had a

Victory Garden, rolled bandages, and gave socials and open houses at our Temple for the soldiers. I remember one cold day there was a meeting of the Jewish soldiers' wives at our Temple. The building was still heated by a coal furnace and Marvin came down to stoke the furnace. One of the northern girls asked me if my husband was the janitor. "No," I told her truthfully, "he's the president of the congregation." Our Sisterhood helped with the Seders at Camp Sibert. The Chaplain was a fiercely Orthodox Rabbi. Everything had to be strictly kosher. At one work session, Rose Greenberg accidentally dumped a whole can of kerosene (mistakenly marked salad dressing) into a mountain of salad. The Rabbi's wife had to walk miles from their house in Attalla to the camp on Shabbat and Holy Days.

One year, some of the girls and I planned to have a Seder at our house. They knew a lot more about cooking and preparing food than I did, especially Adele Keller from St. Louis. They wanted to make gefilte fish and we all worked very hard. When the gefilte fish was almost done, in came Abe Shugerman's mother from next door. She tasted the broth and promptly added salt. Result – the fish was too salty. When I told Mama what happened she told me not to worry. Just boil up more water seasoned with carrots and onions and cook the fish in the new liquid. It worked and the day was saved. Apparently gefilte fish cannot be overcooked.

World War II was a ghastly time. There was so much tragedy. We did know something about how the Jews in Europe were suffering, but not the horrors of the Holocaust. I can still hear Hitler's voice as he addressed the thousands of Germans in Berlin. Though I didn't know German, it was easy to understand the word "Jude" as Hitler harangued his audience and they shouted back their agreement and their Heils. Just hearing all this over the radio was blood chilling. There were already German and Austrian refugees in Birmingham, welcomed and some supported by the Jewish community. The Gadsden Jewish community, too, tried to do its part. Our refugee family was from Austria. They were Mr. and Mrs. Gronich and their teenage daughter. Mr. Gronich had worked in a bank in Austria. In Gadsden he became the night watchman at Atlas Iron and Metal Company. That was the only job available. Mr. Gronich would go to work every night with his briefcase. Now it was carrying his evening meal or snack. Iron contracts and expands according to the temperature and makes a noise. This was a source of discomfort and fear for Mr. Gronich. The family finally moved away to a larger city. I was pregnant with Alfred at this time and it was Mrs. Gronich who told me that Alfred would be a very nice name for a little son. So I remember her with some gratitude.

Alan now left Vanderbilt University and joined the air corps. He ended up serving in India and got home safely after the war. Even Yank served in the Army and fought in Italy. Izzy was in the infantry. He became a captain, but before that he fought in the Battle of the Bulge and in taking the famous bridge into Remagen, Germany. He was wounded and was awarded the Purple Heart twice, but he got home safely and well. How blessed we were! Marvin's cousin, Joel Sater, served in the Navy, but I really don't know the details of his service. Cousin Robert Jacobs was in the Navy.

Linda Gail was born July 1, 1945. She was a little baby when we got word that the war was over. It all felt like a dream as I remember it. Although Marvin tried his best to get drunk that night, I'm not sure he did.

Through the years Marvin was always sentimental about our marriage. He was the one who had our Ketuba (marriage contract} framed and hung in a prominent place. He was the one, too, who wanted to celebrate our 40th wedding anniversary with a large family dinner party at the Gadsden Country Club. It was a lovely affair and one to remember. But then, when our 45th wedding anniversary approached, he instigated plans to celebrate that, too. We decided to combine our anniversary with a family reunion. Arrangements were made to hold a weekend of affairs at the Guntersville State Park. Rooms at the large Guntersville Inn were reserved. Also, several chalets were booked. All our family, on both sides, were invited and they responded with enthusiasm. In the midst of all these happy plans, we were informed of Marvin's serious illness. It wasn't easy for us but we decided to go along with our original plans. And we did. The family came to Guntersville from far and near. It was a bittersweet time for a lot of us. However, I'm sure everyone was glad that they attended. The next year a number of our family members left us, including Marvin.

Alfred and Linda Gail

I want to tell you more about the birth of Alfred and the beginning of our life as a family. As I mentioned earlier, Alfred was born in 1942 during Passover. When I called Marvin at work he drove an old car home because I had our car and after he rushed me to the hospital, we never found the keys to that old car again. My doctor got to the hospital promptly, but left soon after not to be found again. Sarah and Jake had driven up to Gadsden from Birmingham. When Sarah saw I was about to deliver in my room at the hospital, she went downstairs and dragged the owner of the hospital, Dr. Rawls, up to see me. But he was too late. Alfred had already arrived into this world. I guess he decided to take matters into his own hands and get it done. Thank God he was fine and healthy and beautiful. Later, we did have some trouble getting him fed correctly. After we took him to Birmingham to Dr. Chapman, he blossomed and became an adorable pleasure to everyone and of course, very bright.

Marvin had a swing set built for our back yard. It was a special one for young children that had a seat with a back and a safety bar across the front. We also had a sandbox under a large tree. In those days, children came to our yard from all over the neighborhood. Alfred's crib was upstairs, so we used our nice buggy for his naps. When he began to walk, we had a gate built for our front porch. He was about three- years old when we'd sit at the living room window or on the front porch waiting for "Daddy" to come home.

Alfred could tell me the name of every car driving past our house. If he was wrong, I didn't know the difference. He loved his little cars and slept with them in his bed.

Alfred was about two or three when I made him a costume for Halloween. I never did know how to sew, but this time I copied his pajamas in red cloth and made a devil costume. I stuffed the long tail with cotton and sewed it on the back of the pants. On our second stop, which was at the Shugarman's, we were going up the front steps when I accidentally stepped on the tail and off it came. He didn't mind at that age, some "little devil." All the neighbors knew Alfred since, in those days, we thought fresh air was great for children. We would take him for walks in his buggy, then stroller and then on his own. I still remember the first time someone asked me if I was Alfred's mother. It was a brand new identity.

Between the birth of Alfred and Linda I had miscarried. Soon I became pregnant with our little girl. I have always felt that the miscarriage was for the best. And I remember mostly how Marvin brought Alfred down across the street from the Holy Name of Jesus Hospital so he could wave to me and I could see my little boy. Children weren't allowed in hospitals in those days. Carrying Linda I saw another doctor, Ralph Clark. He was using a new saddle block which was supposed to make the delivery painless. When birth time came, the nurses at Forrest General Hospital remembered me and saw that my doctor didn't leave the hospital. Remembering what happened when Alfred was borne three years earlier, they were really nervous. True to form we didn't have time for the "new procedure." Thank God our little Linda arrived healthy and beautiful, but I have regretted that the doctor gave me DES to prevent miscarriage, and I can't help wondering if that DES was the root of her illness later.[5]

Now we had a lovely family and a happy life. Right before Linda's birth Marvin decided to sell Atlas Iron and Metal Company and get out of the scrap

---

[5] Diethylstilbestrol (DES) was given to women from 1938 to 1971, ostensibly as a way of preventing miscarriages. In 1971, the FDA banned the drug after it was discovered the cause a rare form of cancer, as well as birth defects and other health problems.

business. Alan was away in the service, and Ethel was in New York married to Sam Green and living the life of a wealthy Easterner. When Marvin talked, or maybe wrote, to Alan about the change he was told, "Go ahead and do whatever you like. I'm not there and anything you do is okay with me." So Marvin went ahead and sold the company. Marvin had been in the business since he was a kid, and he had learned how to bid on scrap. He now used this knowledge to bid on government surplus.

When Linda was born, Marvin wasn't working. However, we kept our practical nurse for three weeks instead of two so we could do some things together. She was a good baby, and we knew a little more than we had with our first. I remember Marvin took Alfred to the hospital so he could ride home in the ambulance with me and his new little sister. We bent over backwards to keep him from feeling neglected. He took seriously his position of big brother and was quite paternal.

With all the boys on Marvin's side, our little girl was most welcome. She didn't have much hair the first two years. Then it came in ringlets. When strangers would stop to tell me what a beautiful little "boy" she was I would be really put out. Couldn't they see how feminine she was? And she really was. Linda Gail was named after Marvin's grandmother Lena Jasvoin Lipzitz, and Uncle Label's wife, Gittel. Gittel was an unusually fine and sweet person. One was very strong and the other very gentle and sweet. As Linda matured, she showed qualities of both of these remarkable women.

I don't think that I've told you about Jessie Garry. Jessie taught me one of the most important lessons of my life, not that she had any college degrees that I know about, but she must have been worldly wise. This all happened when we lived on Chestnut Street. Linda Gail was a small child and Robert hadn't been born yet. So Alfred was very young too. Jessie helped me around the house. One morning she came in and was working in the kitchen when I came scurrying in and began telling her what all I had to do that day-bake a cake and work in the flower garden and attend a meeting, etc. Well, Jessie who had probably been up since dawn taking care of her own family and probably washing clothes before coming to our house, told me, "The only way to get anything done is to start doing!" That stopped me in my tracks. But throughout my life since then, I've considered it one of the most valuable lessons that I've ever learned. And I really start "doing," even when I'm not sure how to go about doing some task and it usually works out fine.

Around this time, my sister Pauline moved to Gadsden. After she and Sam got married, they lived in Greensburg, Indiana where both of their older children, Stanley and Marcia, were born. However, Sam wanted to make a change because he was working as a manager and preferred having his own store. It just so happened that a Mr. Jacobson was trying to sell his men's clothing store and move from Gadsden, so Sam bought the store. Pauline and I were together in the same town and how wonderful that was for me. Pauline was always a dear big sister, never bossy at all, but helping us as much as she could. Having my sister Pauline and her family in Gadsden made life very warm and good. We saw each other or spoke on the phone everyday.

Pauline's younger children, Eddy and Rosalie, were born in Gadsden. Alfred and Stanley were just a few months apart in age and grew up as very close cousins. Robert and Eddy were born about a month apart. Marcia was a little older than Linda Gail. And Rosalie, the youngest, has always been everyone's favorite. I'm sure all our children loved and enjoyed their cousins. Howard Sarasohn used to come to visit. I don't remember Adele, his sister, coming except with the family. She was a little older, so I guess that's why.

I do have to tell you about Marvin and Mr. Jacobson. Marvin had learned to play chess and Mr.

Jacobson was his teacher. We had a new baby and spent most evenings at home. Mr. Jacobson would come over several nights a week to play chess with Marvin. Marvin got beat every night for a long time, but finally, one evening Marvin actually won the game. The next night Mr. Jacobson telephoned for a return match. When he arrived at our house on Chestnut Street that night, he looked terrible. He was haggard, with dark circles under his eyes and told us he hadn't slept a wink all night trying to figure out what had gone wrong. Thank heavens, Mr. Jacobson won that night. I don’t know whether or not Marvin lightened up on his game or his teacher just took full control.

Marvin got to be a good chess player and taught Alfred and especially Robert. While I’m talking about chess I might as well tell you about the time Robert was about seven and ill enough to be kept in bed before TV was a “nurse.” I’d been playing games with Robert all morning, keeping him in bed until our pediatrician, Dr. Amos Gipson, could see him. I’d resorted to a chess game even though I wasn’t very good. Finally, Dr. Gipson arrived and checked Robert out; I think he had a sore throat. When Dr. Gipson spotted the chess board, he decided to play a game with Robert. I told the doctor that I knew he was too busy and didn’t have to do that. He said, “Oh I used to play chess with my boys; it won’t take long.” Well, about 45 minutes later he was still in there and hadn’t beaten Robert yet. I can’t remember who finally won, but they had a good game. Robert was so fond of Dr. Gipson. Later, Dr. Gipson moved to Tuscaloosa. When Robert was down at the University of Alabama, he went to visit his old pediatrician many times. But I'm getting ahead of myself.

Marvin's Hardware and Building Materials Company

After Marvin closed Atlas Iron and Metal, he was looking for some other business. Army-Navy stores were flourishing and there wasn't one in Alabama City. He started looking for a location there and found one on Wall Street. Republic Steel Company was located in Alabama City, as was a large cotton mill called Dwight Mills, which later became Cone Mills. In addition to these big companies, there were about six clothing stores, a furniture store, a bakery, two drug stores, a bank and other small businesses. All seemed to be thriving. Nearby was Attalla with a large pipe shop and other mills. We furnished the store with very little outlay. Marvin bought used shelves from Camp Sibert and tables from a Gadsden store going out of business. This store was owned by Nathan Goldstein who had decided to move his family to Birmingham.

Grandpa Reuben helped paint the shelves while Marvin was out of town buying. The first stock consisted of army surplus and contained some good buys. The hose bibcock faucets went like hotcakes as there were none available from regular hardware suppliers. Articles of that kind brought in money and army surplus clothing was selling, too. However, Marvin had no experience in the dry goods business, and after a few weeks he told me he was selling all that clothing to an army surplus store in Anniston. And he did that very weekend. So, we were left in the hardware business. All the established hardware stores were on allotment from Birmingham wholesalers like Moore & Handley and Wimberly & Thomas, so Marvin went to New York to buy.

Some friends of Sam Green told him where to go on New York's Lower East Side. There, he had help from a Jewish firm by the name of J.J. Korn. Mr. Korn sold him a very complete and good variety of tools and hardware items. There were others who helped, too. The order of tools came in to Marvin's Hardware and Marvin and I were working long hours to get our new business ready to open. Late one night, maybe early morning, we were marking those tools from Mr. Korn and we finally got them all marked but two – an adz and a wedge according to the invoice. We didn't know which was which and couldn't agree. That brought on one of the biggest arguments of our marriage. Those darn tools didn't sell and stayed on the shelf for years.

Marvin's soon got a reputation for having what people were looking for. Marvin continued to buy from his sources in New York and also from Belknap and Company in Louisville, KY. Mr. Brumback, their salesman, became a good friend and remained so for many years. The business grew and soon added housewares and plumbing fixtures and supplies to their inventory. When Alan returned from WWII, he went right to work. These two brothers were really hard workers and good businessmen, while I did the office work until we were finally able to hire a bookkeeper. The business was successful and before too long, took in the building next door. The next expansion came in the form of a warehouse across the street.

The housewares department grew from mostly enamelware to stainless steel and electrical appliances. Marvin's opened a toy department for Christmas business and soon rented a store across the street to turn into a seasonal toy store. Marvin and Alan kept this up for a few years and the toy store was successful, but they got tired of having to put together big items like bicycles and trying to get all the toys delivered by Christmas.

Plumbing supplies and plumbing fixtures became a big part of the business. Sewers were being installed all around the Alabama City area, and people were putting in new bathrooms and kitchens. Alan and Marvin found sources for "seconds" in that line in

Massachusetts, and soon they were buying by the truckload. The days of making deliveries with the little trailer attached to the back of our car were over. Marvin's began using trucks to deliver big items like plywood and other building and electrical supplies. As the building supply department flourished, another service was added. The old railroad station in Alabama City became the location for the manufacturing of door units and window units. Pledger Moore, a fine person and talented mechanic, designed the equipment for this venture which supplied Marvin's stores. It was later enlarged at a new location. This became the Marval Company and subsequently, Coosa Mill Works, which now manufactures a variety of door units for general sales. On Saturday mornings, lots of Alabama City folks would go in to Gadsden to shop. Once the family moved to East Gadsden, we saw how busy downtown Gadsden was compared to Alabama City. Finally, the brothers decided to open a second Marvin's store on Broad Street in Gadsden. The location was on the same block as Southern Hardware, a long established Gadsden business. A half-block away in the other direction was Gadsden Hardware, a wholesale dealer with exclusive rights to sell all nails (and perhaps other products, but I'm not sure) made by Republic Steel. The first few months in the new store were very slow and very hard. Some days the total sales were only $35. Marvin developed an ulcer, but in spite of that and by the pure force of his personality and hard work, the downtown store finally prospered and enlarged to take in the store next door. Alan remained in Alabama City and worked hard and was a good businessman, so both stores were doing very well. The public liked both Alan and Marvin and felt good about dealing with them. They sold many a bathroom and kitchen bought through FHA, a legacy of the Roosevelt programs created to make it easier for people of moderate means to secure loans.

Many years later, the Cohn brothers began to think of combining both stores at a new address where they could have a large store with a large lumber yard, and they wanted it to be on a railroad siding. The first shopping center in Gadsden was built in 1960 on 12th Street South. It was a strip shopping center with some big stores and the A&P (then my favorite grocery store). The Cohns found a location on South 11th Street not far from the shopping center. It had plenty of room for parking and any eventual growth. The Gadsden store was located there until recently. By this time the business had become known as Marvin's Hardware and Building Supply Company. Under Alfred's progressive leadership and later ownership, Marvin's Building

Materials and Home Centers Company (as it is now called) has grown and become a fair- sized chain with around twenty-five branches in three states at this writing. But, I'm getting way ahead of my story...

Gadsden's Other Townsfolk

Since this is, after all, a "memoir," I suppose I should tell you something about my thoughts on a few subjects not directly related to my family. I grew up with great respect for our democratic system of government and viewed the U.S. as truly a "classless society." Brought up by a gentle and loving family and rather sheltered from the outer world and ugly parts of existence, I still felt that I knew the realities of life. The history and circumstances of my parents, who were immigrants from Russian oppression, and also struggled through the Great Depression, were not lost on me. Also, I was ever aware of my Jewishness and our struggle for acceptance. Still, I knew that there were American Jews in high places in the government and in the business world and we also had great writers and scientists, composers and musicians. We were all Jews, but weren't all alike. I knew even then that some people were better educated, more cultured and much richer. There were even some so anxious to appear genteel that they spelled it "gentile" in a grand effort to be accepted. Still, in my heart's heart, I knew that the values I had learned from my parents were what really mattered. And I thought that honesty, integrity, and compassion were traits that counted with most Americans in our "classless society." For some unfathomable reason, the black population was of only marginal importance in this equation. I wonder now at the general thoughtless acceptance of the unfair and immoral status quo to which this large segment of our society was subjected. In the '60's I did serve on a bi-racial committee sponsored by Frank Helderman, Jr., publisher of the *Gadsden Times*. Later, Marvin served on a bi-racial committee sponsored by the mayor of Gadsden. This small beginning did not result in great change. However, I think it did soften and improve the relation between the races.

It wasn't until the 1940's that I discovered what my wise young husband already knew. The U.S. did have an under class of poor whites. This knowledge came to me in the form of a large wreck of a man called Spit Red. (I shudder to think how he got that name.) Robert remembers this man's real name. It was McElduff. That in itself tells us something about the difference in generations. I first saw Spit Red when he was working on a garbage truck in our neighborhood. It happened that Marvin and I were out with our little boy, Alfred, when the garbage truck stopped on the corner and Marvin hailed Spit Red.

Gadsden was a small town so people often met on the streets. Also, Marvin had probably had some dealings at Atlas Iron and Metal Company, our former business, where some poor people brought in scrap iron and even rags to sell for a bit of cash. This was before we had to pay people to recycle our paper, cans and other refuse; sometimes these folks pulled hand-drawn wagons and carts on which they had gathered salable items. They were trying their best to earn a few pennies. Most of these unfortunate people lived on the edge of the city in a place called Hoover Town – a bitter reference to our president during those hard times. Hoover Town was a collection of shacks and it was probably in the backwoods. Places like this were abandoned after federal housing projects were established. Housing projects may not look so good now, but compared to the pitiful housing available to the poor at that time, these apartments were not just a haven, but almost heaven.

Being the kind of person he was, Marvin gave some of these folks a friendly hand from time to time. One of these people named Gertrude came by Marvin's Hardware regularly for a handout and a friendly word. She probably wasn't very old. Her appearance mirrored her hard life. She was painfully thin, had no teeth, and wore ragged clothes and worn shoes. Her hair was not yet grey but was colorless and unkempt. No matter, she always smiled her toothless grin when she greeted "Mr. Marvin." Once when she came by our downtown store and complained about having no food, Marvin picked up the phone and called the big Piggly Wiggly Grocery down on the corner of Broad Street. He told them, "I'm sending my girlfriend to your store. Give her all the groceries she wants and charge them to me." He knew the clerks would be excitedly waiting for Marvin's girlfriend and hardly able to refrain from the joy of spreading this "scandal" around Gadsden. Well, they all got a good laugh when they saw Gertrude, but she was happy with her haul of groceries.

When Robert came into the business, he always had time for these people, too, but he seemed to have a more personal relationship with them. He once took a black derelict into the restaurant near our office. The owner, never known to be broad-minded, could do nothing but have them both served. Cold days would find Spit Red sitting in a corner of Robert's office wearing one of Marvin's cast-off, tailor-made (Finchley) jackets and nodding in the good warmth. Often a high-powered salesman or manufacturers' rep came by to call on Robert while Spit Red was sitting there. These men might have wondered about the situation, but never got an explanation. They probably got an introduction, though.

I don't know what happened to Gertrude. But I do know about Jeanette Turly. One cold day Robert found her shivering on the road to Alabama City. She was a step above Gertrude. Her brother-in-law sold apples from his bicycle downtown. "He was the best of the lot," Jeanette told Robert. As she got older and less able to take care of herself, Robert saw that she became a resident of a very nice nursing home on the mountain in Gadsden. He kept up with Jeanette, visited her and sometimes took her on outings. When the nurses had a problem with Jeanette – she often refused to let them bathe her – they would phone Robert for help. Once, Robert brought Jeanette to Birmingham and to Lee Rogoff's store to make a few purchases. A couple of weeks later, I saw Lee and he told me about that visit. "I thought I knew everyone in the family," said Lee, "and I wondered, who in the hell is that?" When Jeanette died in the nursing home, her family, finally, showed up to see if she had left anything of value. I remember Robert sent me to the nursing home on an errand concerning all of this.

There were other people we would see now and again on the streets of Gadsden. They were struggling to keep alive and hardly equipped for the present or the future. In a larger city I think residents are more isolated, staying within their own groups. In a smaller place it's very different. Though we still spend most of our time with our own social and or religious group, personal contact with strangers is a matter of course. We see that life isn't like a TV presentation. There are other people out there, people with their own priorities and problems, their own luck, and their chances in this life. No, I found out that this isn't really a "classless society" here in the U.S. We aren't all created equal nor are we all born with the same chances for a good life. Destiny can sometimes dictate our place and that can influence how it all plays out.

Family Life: Now Including Robert

Just as our business life was developing and expanding, so was our life at home. Linda was just five months old when we opened the first store in Alabama City. I worked regularly then and have always felt I should have spent more time with her. When I start thinking about Linda I have so many regrets that I find it hard to write. But I do think she was a happy little girl. When we had her play house built, Marvin told me, "I guess you're happy now – you probably always wanted a playhouse." It really was a nice one, big enough to stand up and walk around in with a nice little front porch with banisters. Linda never really cared much about keeping her playhouse clean or neat. Her little friends would come over and clean up the place. When Robert was a little boy, he and his friends would climb out the windows and on the roof and play cowboy. Linda was a good student and popular. When she started the first grade at Donahue School, I stayed outside the room in the hall worrying about leaving her that first day. She finally glanced up and saw me looking in the door and motioned for me "to go on home" and that was that. She was independent and not my shy little baby girl after all.

The years rushed by, now that I think of it. Linda was a fine little intelligent girl, kind and gentle, but strong too. She became that kind of woman. The 10 years we lived in East Gadsden she developed – took dancing lessons and piano and made good friends at school. Now I wonder if she got enough attention the years Robert was a sick little boy and I was so busy taking care of him.

Robert was born in 1948. We still lived on Chestnut Street. This time I went to a real obstetrician and had good care. As usual the labor was not long, and he was a fine strapping baby. By this time, with two older children, I felt more in charge – and still remember the joy of rocking Robert and nursing him while he was growing and gaining. I did notice he had an unusual amount of diarrhea. When I spoke to the pediatrician, he suggested I stop nursing. That was a mistake. After we put him on a bottle, he started losing weight and we thought something was really wrong. We changed formulas several times to no avail.

Finally, we took him to Birmingham to Dr. Hughes Kennedy III who sent Robert to Children's Hospital. There were no private rooms available so I wasn't allowed to stay with him. When I was allowed to visit my child, he would lift up his arms to be picked up. One day a young doctor told me to "pick up my baby." When I did the nurse wouldn't allow it. So I'd stay outside the nursery door and cry and Robert went on a "hunger strike."

Finally, Dr. Blank, a Gadsden friend, came in and suggested we take our baby to Boston's Children's Hospital. Before we left, Izzy gave Robert a blood transfusion. We must have flown on a small plane because Izzy had to bring ice on board to pack the baby's bottles. When we got to the hospital in Boston, I told our doctor I'd have to stay with my baby. He agreed to allow me to stay all day, but not to spend the night. Marvin was the most supportive husband and father a person could have. He looked after me while Ethel came to Gadsden and stayed with Alfred and Linda.

The doctor in Boston always held our baby gently in his hands while doing his examination. They started giving this little patient liver shots and it always took about three people to hold him down, even then when he was so thin with a bloated stomach (like a starving child) with great big eyes. But he seemed to be improving. Dr. Kennedy's son was at this hospital and very nice to us. In about a week, we were allowed to leave and went home with a special diet and instructions. Our room on the train was hung with wet diapers. And when we got home – buying ripe bananas became an important task.

Robert just about lived on bananas, skim milk, and no fats whatsoever. He began to blossom, but didn't ever completely get over the diarrhea. This trouble was called Celiac Disease and should have been cured by diet. We used a doctor in Gadsden, but still took Robert to see Dr. Hughes Kennedy, III in Birmingham at regular intervals. When Robert reached about two years of age, I took him to Dr. Kennedy and he gave me an article to read about celiac disease. It was written by Dr. Sidney Valentine Haas who had discovered the banana cure for celiac. I took the article home and after Marvin and I had read it we talked it over and decided we'd like to take Robert to New York to see Dr. Haas.

Dr. Kennedy was enthusiastic about our idea and made all the necessary arrangements. We took an apartment about a block from Dr. Haas' office which he shared with his son, Dr. Merrel Haas. Dr. Haas was a tall distinguished man with white hair and a gentlemanly manner. At first he wanted to put Robert in the hospital and when I told him about my experience in Birmingham, he told me they'd get me uniforms and I could stay with Robert as a nurse. He then changed his mind and thought he could just see Robert in his office everyday and we would live nearby for about 10 days.

We took this nice old, large apartment somewhere on Central Park West. We would take Robert to Central Park every day to play and when the weather was bad, we'd go to the Museum of Science close by. Usually the museum was full of children so we didn't have to worry about our child running about and making a little noise.

Rex Sater was in New York then trying to get into the theater. His home was in a cold-water flat, but he never let us see where he lived. He came to see us and even kept Robert one night so we could go out. We were in New York in November, 1952 when Adlai Stevenson was defeated for President of the United States by Dwight D. Eisenhower. Marvin, Rex, and I were devastated.

Our neighbors across from the back of our apartment walked around naked all the time so we kept our shades drawn. We loved being with Rex, as I still do. Dr. Haas changed Robert's diet and allowed him to have fat. Robert especially loved bacon and Dr. Haas told us not to be surprised at the amount of bacon Robert would eat as his body was starved for fat. We went home with this new diet. Still no carbohydrates were allowed, but a new milk product, protein milk, was prescribed instead of skim milk. We were to continue this for a year and then come back to see the doctor.

After a year Robert had improved a lot, but was not completely recovered. That time finally came, but he still had some allergies and diet problems. On our second trip to New York we went by car and my sister Pauline and her little boy Eddy went with us to see a famous ophthalmologist about Eddy's eye. Robert and Eddy fought the whole trip no matter what Pauline and I did. When we got home Marvin went right to the hospital with one of his famous backaches.

Eddy's report wasn't encouraging, but it did give his parents guidance. After a few months, Robert began to lose all the celiac symptoms, but he was allergic to some foods and usually his "stomach" was the problem. By the time Robert started school he was pretty much normal and always behaved like a regular little boy, loveable, well liked, and a pleasure to us at home. Alfred probably should get credit for this because he never let Robert get away with anything and kept him from developing into a "spoiled and pampered" fellow. Linda was always very maternal toward Robert. They continued to have a very close and special relationship even as grown-ups. Robert grew into a strong and independent person, never afraid to venture into new places and try different lifestyles.

East Gadsden

In 1950, we bought a house in East Gadsden at 229 S. 9th Street. Uncle Label lent us some money so we could buy this house and have it remodeled into a very comfortable, but not overly large, home. Marvin would never have a mortgage on his home because he remembered how his family lost their lovely home in Birmingham during the Depression. We paid Uncle Label regularly. When he died his will declared the balance on the loan, still a few thousand dollars, paid in full as a gift for us.

Our new home was in a nice neighborhood. We were just a block from our friends, the Harwoods, and Donahoo Elementary School was located within walking distance. We enlarged the house and rebuilt the kitchen. It was a comfortable house with a screened porch on the front. A very large oak tree shaded the porch all summer and the children played games (and fought over them) and entertained friends there, too. Our house was on a corner lot. The back yard was very large and became like a playground for the neighborhood. The yard was so large that when we bought the house we thought of building another house to rent out on the back of our lot, but we never did. We put in basketball rims and a swing set. We also fenced in an area for our dog (really Alfred's) named Lucky, and Linda's play house had a nice spot under a cottonwood tree.

I remember a neighbor, two doors down on 9th Street. She was a widow and really didn't want Lucky in her yard. One day she said to me, "Your children don't ever go to their friends to play, do they?" This was Southern for, "All those children in your backyard everyday are getting on my nerves."

Linda was a conscientious student and took piano lessons and dancing lessons. Marvin almost always managed to have a "backache" at recital time so he had an excuse to leave early, right after Linda's performance. Two hectic experiences at dance recital time are etched in memory. First, the zipper on Linda's costume broke right before time to leave for the recital. The next year, when I went to pick up her costume the day of the recital, I found the dressmaker hadn't even begun to sew it up. Mrs. Lyda, our neighbor, came to the rescue, while I left Linda soaking in the tub and relaxing before the big event. Her solo dance came off without a hitch. She was a cute little Red Riding Hood and, of course, the costume was red satin.

When we lived in East Gadsden we had a nice social life. Arthur Berman had remarried to Lee and we had a supper club and played cards with other couples, some younger and some older, as people do in a small town.

Russia- Malkin grandparents- Chaya Pesha and Hatzkel surrounded by daughters. Left to right: Channah, Clara, Bashia, Chasia, Ita and Slava in front. Picture made about 1910 after Mama (Dascha) and Uncle Monya had already immigrated to U.S.

Papa with sister Rose - before both immigrated to U.S. Sister-in-law Esther in center.

Grandmother Adella Euchvitz

Papa (Jacob Euchvitz) as a young man.

Papa's brother Avram Hershel and wife Esther with children - early 1900's

My Parents

Beloved parents in their middle years - Birmingham

My Future Husband Marvin Cohn

Four generations : Grandpa Reuben Lipsitz, Ethel Cohn holding Marvin, Great grandfather Louis Lipsitz----Birmingham

Mother (Ethel Lipsitz) with baby Marvin----1919

Marvin at about 5 years of age

Marvin's family: Grandmother Lena Jasvoin Lipsitz

Marvin's mother (Ethel Lipsitz) and father (Abe J. Cohn) on becoming engaged to be married in Savannah, GA

Anne and Marvin - Sunday afternoon stroll near Highland Park - 1939

Anne and Marvin about 1938 at Guntersville Lake

Marvin and Anne

Honeymoon, 1940

Twenty-fifth Wedding Anniversary - 1965

Fortieth Wedding Anniversary -1980

Forty-fifth Wedding Anniversary

Fortieth Anniversary celebration with family

Family Life: Now Including Robert

Children - Alfred, Linda Gail and Robert about 1950

Our Family Grows

Alfred and Linda Cohn with children
Martin Joseph, Michael David and Daniel Eric

Linda and John Speaks with Jacob Aaron
and John Thomas III

Eileen and Robert Cohn with Philip David
and Abbey Lauren

Great Grandchildren

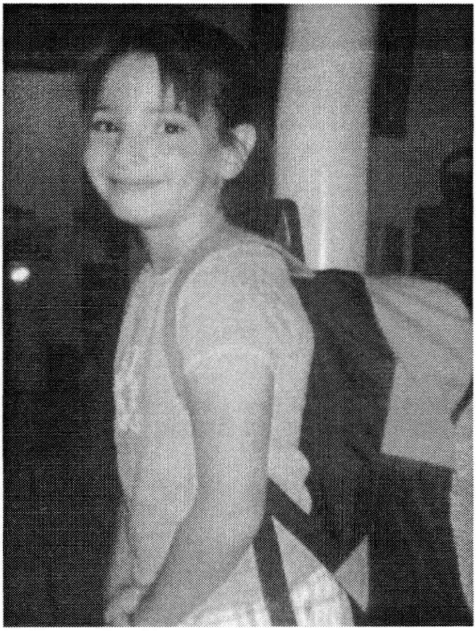

Olivia Gabrielle Cohn (2008)

Joshua Meyer Cohn holding Samuel Thomas Cohn (2008)

Morgan Russell (2008)

John T. Speaks IV (2008)

Fairoaks

Our home at 143 Fairoaks in Gadsden

Living room with Linda Gail and John

Remembering Happy Times and Losses

Sam Green passed away in 1953 after he and Ethel had been married for 10 years. Soon, Ethel moved back to Gadsden where she and Alan shared an apartment. Later, Ethel married Leopold Schoenberg and moved to Beaufort, SC. For Ethel it was a homecoming, as Beaufort was only 40 miles from Savannah where the Lipsitz family lived before moving to Birmingham and where she grew up. Ethel knew Beaufort and that part of South Carolina well and had relatives scattered around the area. She was really happy there. After Leopold passed away, Ethel returned to Gadsden once more where she lived until age 96.

In June of 1955, Alan married Charlotte Jospin. Charlotte was from Bessemer. Charlotte and I really became like sisters. We celebrated holidays together and made large Seders for Passover – inviting students from Gadsden Junior College (at one time there were a number of Jewish boys from Iran at the school because of the language lab) and other unattached people. When Marvin's aunt and uncle, Freda and Jack Cowan, and their niece, Harriet, all moved to Gadsden our family flourished.

My sister, Sarah, and her husband, Jake, lived in Bessemer at this time. They had a small business Jake had bought from his brother-in-law, Felix Shevinsky, after WWII. It was during these days that Sarah became ill. She had already undergone a mastectomy and was recovering nicely, but then during the next year developed acute leukemia. She was hospitalized right after Alan and Charlotte's wedding. Sarah was so pale at the wedding. She must have made an heroic effort just to get dressed and attend. The acute Leukemia was incurable then and even untreatable. She only lived two weeks after being diagnosed. She had been such a beautiful woman, so full of vitality with a special "spark" in her nature. Sometimes she spoke her mind rather quickly, but her friends loved and respected her, probably because of her complete honesty, straightforwardness, and good heart. Even though he married a few years later, Jake never recovered from the loss of Sarah. Roz, his second wife, tried hard to make her place as a mother to Howard (then about 15) and Adele. She succeeded with Howard but not with Adele. After Jake died at age 49, Howard stayed close to Roz until her death in her 90's. Adele, as much as I know of her, never conquered the bitterness over the loss of her parents. Our loss of Sarah, the first in our family, was a terrible wound that was very slow to heal. Now I understand, since losing my own Linda, how much Mama and Papa suffered. Pauline and Izzy and I tried to keep close to Sarah's children, and I think we did a pretty fair job there.

The loss of Sarah was the beginning of the presence of serious illness and death in my life. Now when I think of it all, I just remember dark clouds of stress and sadness. My heart is heavy with these memories. But I still know in my mind that life can be good and happy at the same time it is just plain rotten. And I finally learned there are some things that must be accepted. We have no power to change what has happened no matter how much we feel sorrow and regret. Pauline, too, was struck with breast cancer. She suffered two mastectomies and finally lost the battle. We lost Papa, too. He was only 75 years old but in those days we thought him an old man.

I read something today about Father's Day (June16th this year) and people were asked to quote some advice given to them by their fathers. So I've been thinking about Papa. I don't remember anything specific he told me – though I'm sure there were times when he shared his thoughts with me. I do remember something he told Izzy when Izzy was leaving home at about age twenty or so to go to work in Huntsville. Papa told his son to "always remember who you are, where you come from and where you're going." I'm afraid Izzy took that advice literally and very lightly – even laughing about it. I know now what good advice that was and wish I could put my arms around Papa and tell him so. I'm afraid I never did tell him how loved he was and how dear to me. Now I know people can learn and be more understanding at any age.

Back to older memories, still not happy ones, but all a part of living. Izzy, too, has left us. He was a devoted brother and family man. In his later years he suffered severe health problems. For a long time he had been living with an ostomy. I never heard him talk as if he felt sorry for himself. In spite of it all and some sort of heart problem, he seemed to be doing all right. He was walking at the mall with friends and socializing with others while faithfully doing volunteer work for the American Ostomy Association. Estelle found him lying on the kitchen floor one morning. That was hard for her, too, as she didn't hear anything during the night. He has been gone since June 1994. That's already ten years as I write this. Even now I just have to think of him to feel his smiling presence.

After Izzy's death my sister-in-law, Estelle, has had lots of health problems. Last week she was directed to start dialysis treatment because her kidneys aren't functioning properly. What a depressing development. She is taking all this better than most people and shows much spirit and courage. She needs to have sitters around the clock and has some good caregivers. Her three daughters and families are showing care and support. As I look back on these times, Estelle has left us after a gallant battle and stoic attitude toward her fate.

Even though I'm the last one alive in my immediate family, all the others, my parents, brother and sisters, still seem very much alive in my memory. Looking back over almost 89 years there is so much to remember and I seem to have forgotten a lot. Then, too, so much has happened in the last twenty years. Soon it will be twenty-two years since Marvin's illness and death.

It didn't seem possible that we would lose Marcia and Stanley Harris at such early ages. Marcia suffered breast cancer and was brave, preparing her children for the inevitable even as she weakened physically. Stanley courageously battled his kidney ailment even going through a kidney transplant to no avail. Their spouses and children have rallied and taken their places in the world. Still these two handsome and gifted young people are remembered and sorely missed

But there are many other losses to remember, also: Sarah, Jake, Papa, Mama, Pauline, Sam, Iz and Estelle, Ethel, her parents and almost all the Lipsitz family. Sadly the younger family members include, Joel Sater, Robert Jacobs and the latest Lawrence Cohn.

All Ethel's generation have gone, too. Her sisters were full of life, sometimes a little wacky, but always interesting and never dull.

For many years I was busy looking after my mother at our house and then in at nursing home. On his deathbed, Papa had told me to take care of Mama and I always did my best. Having such a kind and understanding husband made things easier. He was always good to Mama and she respected him and valued him in return. Pauline was ill during most of those times. Thinking of her suffering brings a dark cloud over my being.

I do find memories of my early family life easier to recall than my own household and times in Gadsden – wonder why? My sisters used to chide me for always asking "why?" growing up, especially when they wanted me to do some chore. Now I finally know there's no purpose in asking "why?" Many parts of living must be accepted without question.

There were happy times between all these losses and one does heal and grow in different ways. As for me, I always had Marvin's concern and love and support. Now back to my lovely children and husband and the days we were all developing into the Marvin Cohn Family.

Growing up in Gadsden

During those days in East Gadsden, Alfred celebrated his Bar Mitzvah. We had a large luncheon at Temple after services and a dinner for the out-of-town guests Friday night and Saturday night. On Sunday we entertained with an open house and reception. It wasn't like the big affairs people have now. For Gadsden, at the time, it was quite elaborate. We were very proud of him. Papa was still alive then and our carrying on tradition meant a lot to him and Mama, too. Of course, Nana came to Gadsden and so did most of the family. Stanley's Bar Mitzvah followed in a couple of months on his birthday.

Alfred went to Disque Junior High School in Gadsden (he and Stanley were in the same grade) but while we lived in East Gadsden, Linda attended Litchfield Junior High. All three of the children attended Donahoo School which was very well run, had good teachers and children from good middle class families. Of course, I was active in the PTA and spent lots of time at the school. So when Robert started he already felt quite at home at Donahoo. During those days I also worked at Marvin's store in Alabama City.

Those 10 years in East Gadsden were good times. Linda was growing into a lovely young girl. Alfred was growing up, too, and experimenting with "grown up" behaviors. We got him a used car at 16, thinking he would like to "tinker" with the motor, etc. Instead, he loaded the trunk with bricks so that it sat low to the ground and I think he liked to "scratch off." When Alfred was about 15 (Marvin was having a hard time with a thyroid condition and was very nervous and high strung) we found out our fine young son was getting a little wild, drinking and getting about with his friends and cousin Stanley. He was doing well in school and really wasn't that bad but we decided to send him off to military school in Georgia. The name of the school was Riverside Academy. One of the drawing points was that the whole school transferred to Hollywood, FL for the winter. But as luck would have it, the Hollywood campus was damaged by a large fire that year and the students were stuck in Gainesville, GA for the winter. Needless to say, Alfred hated that place and I can't tell you how many sleepless nights I spent looking over the school's catalog wondering why we had sent out little boy away to school.

He stayed only one year and then returned to Gadsden High. Marvin had had his thyroid surgery and was back to normal by then. I can't remember if it was before or after Riverside that we had a call from the band director at Gadsden High. On a football trip with the band, some of the boys had gotten too friendly with a group of college boys staying at their hotel and imbibed a bit too much. I'm sure Alfred must have gotten sick because he always did when he drank too much, even in college. Marvin assured Mr. Countryman, the band director, he would take care of Alfred's reprimand. So Alfred had to walk from East Gadsden to Gadsden High for a week or so. I guess he did it because he was always very honest, but he never complained that I know of. He was an active Boy Scout and became an Eagle Scout and Order of the Arrow.

Robert, on the other hand, never took scouting very seriously. When I was the Cub Scout Den Mother all the boys attended regularly, except Robert. I always had interesting projects for them — really. Later, on Scout outings, he'd manage to get his meals at some restaurant or diner. And as for the band, one year the Gadsden High band went on a trip to New York to march in the Macy's Thanksgiving Day Parade. When they returned, I found out Robert and Eddy had been flag carriers and Robert didn't play his instrument at all. And was I furious. After a talk with Mr. Countryman, I think (but wouldn't swear) that Robert returned to his clarinet.

Our Temple is Bombed

On March 25, 1960 our Temple was bombed and Alan Cohn was shot in the aorta. Thank G__ he survived though he still carries that bullet in his body. This all happened on a Friday night. Temple Beth Israel was dedicating a new addition to enlarge the vestry and kitchen and to add Sunday school rooms. This addition was partially funded by Isadore and Daisy Zemmurry. The temple was just about full that night with members and friends from Gadsden, as well as several Zemmurry relatives from Birmingham. I remember the Blouseman family, and there were others. I was Sisterhood President and one of the speakers on this occasion. Marvin had gone to the bus station to pick up Adele Sarasohn (Burnham) so he was going to be late. Our rabbi then was Saul Rubin. He later went to Savannah and wrote a well received history of the old and still functioning temple there.

The service was going on when something hit a window on the 8th Street side of the building. It was a "Molotov Cocktail," but it didn't explode. There was much excitement and I found myself in the Rabbi's study. Suddenly, someone came in and said Alan had been shot. I rushed outside and across the street to the cleaner's lot and found Alan still and ashen in color. I screamed for someone to call 911. They came immediately and took him to the Holy Name of Jesus Hospital. At that time there was no Emergency Room doctor on staff, but a young doctor and surgeon happened to be there seeing or working on a patient. He held Alan's aorta together by hand until Dr. Donald was flown in from Birmingham. The surgery was successful. The bullet was not removed since it had seared the flesh around it and there was no danger of infection. So he's still walking around with that bullet now at age 83. That night was like a bad dream; there were calls from newspapers around the country and friends and relatives in shock. Nana rushed down from her home at the time, someone met her in Atlanta and drove her to Gadsden. Friends, Jew and Gentile, were at the hospital. [6]

---

[6] The following is an excerpt of newspaper article from the New York Times published March 26, 1960.

"A Fire Bomb Strikes Synagogue in the South" By United Press International

Gadsden, Ala., March 25

Three youths hurled a fire bomb against the window of a crowd at synagogue tonight. When several members of the congregation rushed out, we were hit by shots from the youths' car.

One of those hit was hospitalized in critical condition.

Grown men were crying over this devastating and obscene occurrence in our town. The would-be assassin was a 16 year-old high school boy from Attalla. He insisted he acted alone, although several people said they saw more than one assailant. The

---

The incident occurred during a ceremony dedicating a new annex of the Beth Israel Temple. More than 100 persons were present.

State Investigator Harry Sims said the bombing and shooting had been carried out by three teen-agers. Another official said an arrest order had been issued for one of the suspects.

A taxicab believed used by the youths was found abandoned a short distance from the temple. A .22-caliber rifle, more than 20 cartridges, a half gallon can of gasoline, some rags and a machete were found inside.

Police Commissioner M. T. Mashburn said he questioned and released one suspect. The Federal Bureau of Investigation was assisting with the investigation.

Hyman Rosenberg, president of the congregation, said a bottle filled with gasoline and fused by a flaming piece of paper or rag had been thrown at one of the windows. It shattered when it hit the sill and fell outside.

Mr. Rosenberg said several members of the congregation had rushed out to investigate and were greeted by a volley of three shots.

The police identified the two wounded men as Alan Cohn and Alvin Lowi. Mr. Lowi was shot in the hand and apparently not critically wounded. Mr. Cohn, however, was struck in the side and the police said his condition was serious.

police found this boy that night at a small motel in Gadsden. His name was Jerry Hunt. His father was a taxi driver. In his home and in his locker at school the police found Nazi literature and paraphernalia. He was a loner, but we were told he attended the Methodist Church in Attalla regularly. (One of Alan's best friends, Gordon Isbell, and his family belong to that church too. I don't know what conclusion can be drawn there.)

I learned then not to believe everything one reads in the newspaper. There were so many errors in reporting and one long article in particular told about how "Jerry Hunt missed his chess games while being incarcerated." This somehow painted a picture of quite an intellectual young person which was far from the truth and even farther from his background.

Charlotte, of course, was devastated and could never again re-enter her sheltered and idyllic world, but she bore up and held fast to her two little boys. When Jim Martin, a local oil dealer and later state and federal politician, signed bail for this boy's release, Charlotte was, as we all were, very afraid for the safety of the children. Jim Martin was criticized and shunned for this action. When he came by our business to apologize, I don't think Marvin let him off the hook in his usual generous way. I am writing this in as much detail as I can remember because I am becoming one of the last people (besides Charlotte and Alan) to remember how it all came about. I realize that we see everything from our own point of view, but there it is. Thank G__ Alan recovered and doesn't seem to have any after effects from the shooting,

A few days later a solidarity meeting and service was held at Temple Beth Israel. The Anti-defamation League and the American Jewish Committee sent people down to help our congregation and community get through this dreadful time. That service did renew our confidence and appreciation of our neighbors. All the churches took part and the Temple over-flowed into the surrounding streets with well-meaning and sorrowful friends.

I seem to have left out the details of how Alan was shot in the aorta and Alvin Lowi was shot in the hand. These two men ran out the side door of the building to see what had happened and where the bomb came from. The would-be assassin was waiting with his gun across the street for just this opportunity. It was no accident that these two men were involved. They shared some of the same qualities of quickness and hot tempers. I've always felt lucky that Marvin was at the bus station to meet Adele that night because I wonder if he would have had the physical stamina to survive as Alan did.

As the time for the trial approached, we were all tense and wondering if that might bring on more violence from Neo-Nazis and other anti-Semites. No one was looking forward to living it all over again. As it turned out, this case actually never came to trial. One fall day the Attalla High School marching band was practicing at the park on the old Camp Sibert grounds. Jerry Hunt came along in a speeding car and shooting a gun in the air. Whether by accident or on purpose we'll never know, but he drove head on into a large tree and was killed.

I must admit that this was a relief to all involved though a memory had been permanently stamped into our minds and hearts. Rabbi Saul Rubin has written about the Gadsden temple bombing and copies of his book might be secured from the Southern Jewish Historical Society.

In truth, over the years Gadsden has been very welcoming and accepting of its Jewish population. The one exception, many years before our temple bombing, took place in the late 1920's. That's when Mr. Nadler was tarred and feathered and ridden out of town on a rail – courtesy of the Ku Klux Klan. The Nadler Building is still standing on the corner of Chestnut and

5th Street. The Nadler name and date of construction – 1903 – is still quite visible above the entrance. Mr. Nadler, a dignified "Prussian" type, conducted his furniture business in this location. I believe the family was really French. Maybe they were from Alsace Loraine.

The Nadlers were a refined and cultured family. The daughters were good musicians and Mr. Nadler had been an early president of Temple Beth Israel in Gadsden. Pictures of the family show a pleasant home, nicely dressed occupants and a genteel environment. The story goes like this. The Klan was punishing Mr. Nadler because his store had repossessed furniture sold to a "poor widow woman" who couldn't make her weekly or monthly payments on her purchase. This episode forced the closure of Nadler's Furniture Store. The family moved away from Gadsden. I believe some of the children ended up in Birmingham. I heard that one of the Nadler daughters played violin in the Birmingham Symphony Orchestra.

Fairoaks

As with so many times in my life, terrible tragedies were interspersed with moments of beauty and happiness. Nineteen-sixty also saw the realization of years of hard work and the building of the house in which Marvin and I would spend some of our happiest years. Even before we bought our first house in East Gadsden, we had purchased a lot in another part of Gadsden called Clubview. After 10 years in East Gadsden, we built our final home. We had a limited amount to spend, of course, but Marvin really wanted us to have a very nice home. We used an architect from Birmingham, Darcy Tatum, and the builders were the Moon Brothers. Being in the building supply business by that time, we used the finest material we could afford and built a very substantial home. The design was contemporary, split level and fit on our lot. The following is a description I once wrote of my beautiful dream house:

It was meant to be an honest house, a house with no pretensions, and one that would reflect its owners and their family, not some affluent planter's family of pre-civil war days, nor a colonial family of means or even some aristocratic European family of undisputed taste. For the most part, it worked well, though some affectations are evident to the ones who know it best.

The house is designed for today, so as we drive up in our car the house is clearly visible. It is perhaps a little large for the width of the lot, but it was built to fit the sloping land and it does seem to be growing out of the ground. As we walk around the back, we can see that the house is two stories high at one section, but of course, that isn't evident from the front as we drive down the driveway. We park our car in the area which provides room for about four cars with room for each to get in or out without disturbing the other drivers to move their cars. The dry rock wall following one side of the driveway (because the land is higher there) is covered with English Ivy. The trees on the green lawn are mostly pine interspersed with a few oaks - all carefully preserved when the land was cleared for building this house.

The outside of the house is part brick of various shades of tan and brown and part redwood which has been hand rubbed to preserve the original color. The low hanging roof blends with the brick and wood. The entrance is made of two large doors, both of which open to welcome guests. Over the doors glass to the ceiling encourages light to enter the entrance hall. The

Terrazzo floored entrance hall is 12 feet high and extends back about twenty feet to form the hub of the house. From it we may enter the living room or the utility room and kitchen or the stairs leading to the upstairs or the downstairs areas. It is a split-level house with only 6 or 7 steps between each level. Upon entering the house and hanging our coats in the entrance hall closet, we turn left and go down two steps to the large living room. The slanted and beamed ceiling reaches a height of 18 feet on our right where a brick wall 12 feet high and 20 feet long ends in a double fire place which opens into both the living room and the dining room. On our left is a wall of glass. The wall facing us as we enter this room is paneled in oak and continues into the dining room as well. The living room is carpeted and is furnished with comfortable pieces of different styles that blend well together and has some nice accessories and at least one really fine painting on the wall with several good prints. The baby grand piano seems to really belong. It is a soothing environment for contemplation and a comfortable one that lends itself to entertaining small or large groups. The dining room, beamed with high ceilings too, was designed for family use and the floor is covered with a marbleized vinyl which has been somewhat formalized by strips of gold which divides the floor into large squares. A hidden bar opens at the pressure of the hand when conviviality is in order. From the dining room one may enter the kitchen or, as often happens in summer, go out the patio doors to a small porch and then to the stone terrace.

Often the younger members of the family entertain in the downstairs recreation room. We may go there by turning right from the entrance hall and going down the stairs. Here we find a large "L" shaped room – really two rooms with no wall between – part of which has been furnished as a sitting room while the larger part contains a large round table, an old piano, record player and storage for records and games. The dumbwaiter is sent down here from the kitchen above for easy serving of refreshments. The boys' bedroom and bath are also on this floor and how they enjoy their complete privacy. Windows open from all this area to provide plenty of cheerful light.

We return to the hall above so that we may go up the other stairs to the upstairs area where the family enjoys their favorite room, the study. Here the walls are paneled in cherry wood and one wall is lined with books. In this room we find father's reclining chair, the TV, a desk and other comfortable old furniture that the family has lived with so long that it is just a part of being home. Two large bedrooms and two baths are found on this floor, too. One of the bedrooms has, in addition, a dressing room. A very large walk-in closet holds linens as well as cedar-lined drawers for woolens.

Wood paneling is used in much of the house, and the floors are covered with carpeting, wood and cork, ceramic tiles and clay tiles – all materials in which upkeep was considered as important as beauty. Storage space of every kind has been provided for the family's convenience. A large storage space held yard equipment and out door items. Also, the double garage led into the kitchen via the back porch with no stairs to climb with groceries .or just to be covered on rainy days.

But with it all, we will undoubtedly end up in the kitchen with the rest of the family before our visit is over. For the kitchen is the most popular gathering place for the family no matter what the hour. The breakfast area is glass on two sides and affords an unbroken view of the wooded area in the back of the house. The windows show us varying pictures of pine, oak maple and dogwood trees, a bird bath for the pleasure of the birds and squirrels as the seasons dictate.

I've heard that beauty is in the eye of the beholder. Perhaps this house would appear quite differently to someone else. But I hope that you will see it as I do. For this was my house, and I was happy in it.

Annie Bell Garrett

Our neighbors on Fairoaks were George and Frances Pate and their three children. When the Pates decided to hire a white live-in housekeeper from South Alabama, they ended their employment of Annie Bell Garrett. That was really lucky for us Cohns because Bell came to work for us and became a valued member of our family. The Pate's plans didn't turn out so well and they tried to get Bell back, but she refused.

Bell's husband James worked for Republic Steel Corporation, but he had enough time off to do heavy work for Bell at our house and to tend to our yard most of the time. He kept the grounds and did what was needed at The Boathouse, too. Bell was not only a good cook and a dependable and meticulous housekeeper, but she was also a fine seamstress. I never bought any new clothes without consulting her and then she did the necessary alterations. She even made Linda Gail's maternity clothes when that time came.

She was with us for about 30 years, through good times and sorrow and the children's teen and maturing years. I miss and appreciate her part in my life and keep in touch to this day. She and James, her devoted husband, came to Birmingham with me when I moved back from Gadsden, and they helped me get settled in my new home at Carriage Place. All our children, hers and mine, have grown up now and we both have grandchildren and great-grandchildren. James became very ill this past year and died. He was a good friend to me and I know my family remembers them both with affection, too. Years ago, Bell used one of my recipes to prepare a chicken dish that soon became "Bell's Chicken." Sometimes the children try to fix "Bell's Chicken," but it's not like hers – even I don't have her special touch with the seasonings.

My Children Go to College

It was during these times in Gadsden that I took "voice" lessons and later painting. Marvin always encouraged me to develop in every way. He was wiser than I realized at the time. He knew that I always felt deprived of more formal education in spite of voracious reading habits. He loved books, too, and had begun buying books before we were married. I still have many of them, including our large *Webster's 20th Century Dictionary*. It's hard to realize that it is July, 2002, as I write this. Since I was born at the beginning of the 20th century (1919) that has always been my century and I have begun to think about my age and maybe losing my strength and mental abilities as time flies by. I've been lucky so far, but let me get back to the 1960's.

During the busy times when my children were growing up, I did volunteer work for our Temple Sisterhood, the League of Women Voters, the Friends of the Gadsden Public Library, various funds, etc. and was usually "on call" at Marvin's. It wasn't until Alfred came into the business in 1965 that I decided there were enough Cohn's involved and I didn't want to take part any longer.

Alfred was always a good student and a person who looked at the world with realistic eyes. He decided to attend Georgia Tech and study Industrial Engineering. I don't know for sure whether or not he was preparing to go into the family business then, but when he went to Tulane Graduate School for a degree in business and finance, he must have thought about Marvin's. Of course, he could have done well in anything he undertook. I must say, though, that I thought it remarkable that two self-made men like Alan and Marvin respected his judgment enough to put him in a top position. However, I did notice that when Alfred first came into the business, he bided his time, learned as much as he could and didn't try to make changes immediately. But he did work hard and long hours as was the Cohn tradition. I believe Alfred would agree with me that meeting his future wife, Linda S. Lassen was the greatest part of attending Tulane.

Linda Gail chose Tulane, too. She attended the girls' school, Sophie Newcomb, for two years before transferring to Boston University. I think she would say that her college years were happy ones. She spent one summer while at Newcomb at the University of Mexico in Mexico City, and she traveled with the school choir one summer when they gave concerts around that country. She always had a pretty voice and was musical. In high school, she performed a leading roll in South Pacific. When Linda got to Boston University, she saw John Speaks Jr., who was attending Harvard at the time. We thought they were just old high school chums until one night we got a phone call from her telling us that she and John were talking of marriage. Both sets of parents were supportive and they had a happy marriage and produced two lovely sons, John, III and Jacob.

Robert was a "hippie," but that doesn't mean that he ever gave us reason to be disappointed in him. He had all the hair and torn clothes, but he was always very caring and civilized. At least I thought so. After one year at Tulane, where his record was not outstanding but not in the failing range, we decided that we wouldn't send him back and that he could just attend The University of Alabama at Tuscaloosa, a state school with a lower tuition. We thought that he had spent far too much time in New Orleans studying the French Quarter. I've always thought we made a mistake in that. At Tuscaloosa, Robert found all his friends and cronies from Gadsden High and they were mostly rebels. I think he roomed with James Swift and I'm almost sure James took his studies seriously. Eddy Harris had opened a store in Tuscaloosa selling "hippie merchandise." I don't know whether or not he attended classes. At one time, the University allowed students to prepare and present their own classes. Robert was the "teacher" in one. He was very interested in the Civil Rights Movement of this time.

At one demonstration at the University he was arrested, along with the demonstrators, and had to spend the night in jail. When it was time for the trial to come up, Marvin and I drove to Tuscaloosa to do whatever we could. The case was thrown out of court and never came to trial. I didn't know about all Robert's activities. However, I did learn that he had gone to south Alabama to help black people register to vote and stayed with a black family there.

Two times he left for Europe in his ragged jeans and unkempt appearance. Once I took him and Willie Warren, a Gadsden friend, to the highway and another time Robert's Grandmother Nana took him. On the first trip, a nice man picked them up and drove them all the way to Washington, D.C. where he invited them to spend the night at his house. They did, I think.

When he was out of the country, Robert always kept in touch with us. Marvin had requested that. He told Robert, "Be sure to keep in touch because I don't want your Mother waking me at two some morning and telling me I have to go to Europe at once to find you." One time when Robert was in Amsterdam, he sent us a mysterious package to keep for him until he got home. I never opened it, and I'm glad I didn't. Later in life, Robert left his position at Marvin's to establish his own financial consulting business, obtained his B.A. degree and is now, in 2008, doing graduate work at UAB in Human Development. He never tires of learning and his dear wife, Eileen, is an understanding and encouraging helpmate. Certainly, Robert is the best example I know to prove my theory: It takes a little wildness in a boy to make a good man. Robert is surely a fine man. My life would surely be empty without his and Eileen's nurturing and the pleasure and real joy I experience from their two children, Abbey and Philip. They are not only loving, but very interesting people who add a certain new dimension to my days.

True Partners in Every Way

Our little family was very intimate and very loving with an understanding and compassionate father in Marvin. I sometimes have wondered if I didn't expect too much of him. Not that I was a demanding wife as far as material success was concerned. We always used one checking account. Marvin deposited his drawing or salary and we both wrote checks as needed. Sometimes I'd get a few big surprises when checks he'd forgotten to tell me to enter were cleared at the bank.

When he started making investments, Katherine Rampey (the bookkeeper) kept the records. What I later learned, and found quite remarkable, is that Marvin never examined our personal check book. He always seemed to know about what amount we had (though I'd have to figure it all out) and always gave me credit for knowing more than I did.

Marvin never spoke of all he had given me. We were true partners in every way and would never think of distrusting each other. As we grew older, he read someplace that a husband should apprise his wife of all his business. So he put all our investments in my hands, too, not to make the investments, but to keep the records. Later on, he even wrote all the department stores where we had accounts to be sure my name was included in the accounts so that if anything happened to him, I would have an easier transition. My husband really was an unusual person. He was fine and noble, but fun-loving too, and liked to see others enjoy life as well. He was always so good to my family and they certainly loved and respected him.

We had many wonderful trips and always enjoyed each other's company. As we got older he learned to play bridge, even though he had never been a card player. Often we played bridge with another couple, but sometimes just with unattached women like Virginia Willard and Dollie and Rosemary Burke.

Some of our happiest moments took place on the Coosa River. When I caught a prize Big Mouth Bass, Marvin had it mounted, hung it in his office, and felt just as if he had caught it himself. Still, I remember most the pleasure of quiet dusks on the water and the utter contentment of sharing those times.

Israel Connection

Marvin and I made our first trip to Israel in 1968. After that, we returned 5 or 6 more times and always wanted to stay longer. However, we never considered Aliyah. At least I didn't. Marvin may have, but we never discussed it.

While we were in Israel, we met Lila Titova and her daughter Irina. You might recall that Marvin's grandmother was Lena Jasvoin Lipsitz. Lena's younger brother, Abram, was Lila's father. All that family came from Lithuania, and some of our traveling companions had actually remembered knowing Abram in Kaunas. The pictures of this family show very attractive and modern Europeans.

On her mother's side, Lila had a wonderful cousin, who had been a resistance fighter during WWII. Later, at her Kibbutz in Israel, she and her husband, who had also been a resistance fighter, became curators of the Museum of the Resistance and Ghetto Fighters. Visiting the museum was a heart wrenching experience I'll never forget. They had on exhibit the "glass box" from Eichman's trial, as well as maps showing all the "slave labor" plants and sites all over Europe. After looking at all those little lights indicating "slave labor"

I find it impossible to believe the general population was not aware of this going on and the horrible death camps.

Lila had been a teacher in Russia and her husband, Mike, was her school principal. On the first wave of Russian immigration, she and her daughter Irina came to Israel. In order to get permission to leave Russia she had had to divorce her husband. Later, he came to Israel, too, (to join his daughter) and was given an apartment and a pension because he had fought the Nazis. On a trip to the U.S. Joel Sater arranged for Lila and Mike to remarry. We were very fond of Mike and Lila, too, of course. Irina and her husband now live in Pennsylvania, while Lila still lives in Haifa. She is a very devoted Zionist and Israeli, but she may soon move to the U.S. to be closer to family.

Another of our Israel connections is Sarah Lurie Komisar. She is a Sabra and has been our friend since 1967 when she visited Gadsden on an international student program. She and her family have always welcomed us to Israel and we enjoyed knowing her parents, her husband Emanuel, and their three children. They have always added a much valued human element to our visits to Israel.

Israel was always an important part of our lives. In 1983, after the Yom Kippur War, Marvin and I went on a mission to Israel and found a big change in the people we met. They had lost some of their cockiness with the scare of this inexplicable attack. We were later to visit the hospitals where so many Israeli solders were being treated for terrible burns. At the meeting of the people on the mission we pledged more than we'd ever given before, but we felt that nothing else in the world was as important as far as money was concerned. Usually, Marvin and Alan gave together from the business. This time Alan refused to go along so we gave it by ourselves and we got along just as well. Now, as I write this in June, 2002 – the terrible suicide bombings are taking place in Israel – the September 11, 2001, attacks have occurred in the U.S. – and there seems to be so much unrest all over the world.

Anti-Semitism is on the rise in Europe and other places. Now it's called "anti-Israel," but it's still anti-Semitism. Of course, life here in Birmingham is calm and as usual. And I must say my own life is normal. Thank G__ my children and grandchildren are safe. And I just hope and pray the U.S. remains Israel's friend and some of the problems we are facing will be solved.

Grandchildren

Alfred and Linda's son Marty was our first grandchild and we spent lots of time together when the Alfred Cohns lived in Gadsden. I bought "boy" toys and they were kept in a toy box in the large downstairs closet off the play room. Soon, Michael came along and then Dan. Michael probably remembers more about Gadsden than Dan as he was still very young when the family moved to Birmingham. We didn't see each other quite so much with 60 miles between us. But in Gadsden, Linda S. had always welcomed my drop-by visits, unlike one of my friend's daughter-in-law who made a rule that my friend had to make an appointment to visit.

John and Linda Gail's children, Jacob and John III, (Little John) stayed with us in Gadsden many times when they were youngsters. They'd come in by bus and I'd meet these two independent little boys at the bus station. Once, when Jacob was about five or six years old, he and I were throwing a football in the front yard on Fairoaks. All of a sudden, I found myself on the ground. By that night I had developed a terrible pain in my shoulder. Since Marvin usually thought I overdid playing with our grandchildren, I didn't want to tell him about the pain. Finally, though, after trying the electric pad, I had to tell him that maybe I should go to the hospital. He suggested an ice pack and that did give me some relief. The next morning I asked Jacob what had happened. "I think I tackled you, Grandmama," he told me.

Both the Speakes boys loved fishing and "The Boathouse." One afternoon Little John was fishing from the boathouse porch and he caught a prize-size crappie. Marvin had it mounted and kept it hanging in his office. Another day, when Little John and Jacob were about 8 or 10 years old, they were with Marvin and me at the boathouse. As we were all getting ready to take the boat out for some serious fishing, Marvin spotted a dangerous snake coming out of the water and slithering onto the wood supports of the building. He hurried back to the house and brought his rifle. By that time the snake had disappeared so he and Little John went on out in the boat. A short time later, Jacob and I saw the snake coming out of the water and back into the boathouse. "Get the rifle, Grandmama," Jacob told me. When I picked up the rifle, my eight-year old grandson instructed me, "Look through the sight on the barrel of the gun." I did as told, pulled the trigger, and to my astonishment, saw the snake now lying prone on the timber, but minus his head. That was the day

Grandmama became known as a "crack shot" even though it was all beginner's luck

John III and Jacob celebrated their Bar Mitzvahs at Beth Jacob, an orthodox synagogue in Atlanta. They were well grounded in Judaism. The rabbi told us how much he enjoyed these two bright young men.

My grandchildren are an unexpected source of happiness and I do appreciate their allowing me to be a part of their lives now when they are all so busy and working on their present and future plans. I know time is precious to them. (It is for me, too, but for other reasons.) With Arnold and Robert and Abbey, also John III and Susan and Morgan, I attended Marty and Philippa's wedding in England and Jacob and Jennifer's in Houston. How DEAR they are! And now another real miracle. A beautiful great-grandson, Joshua Meyer Cohn is named after Marvin. And a second child is expected in the Martin Cohn household. They will soon be living in the U.S. in Florida.

I remember how great it was to be a part of my grandchildren's lives when they were small. Philip and Abbey came along later and are growing up very fast now. I never got to "keep" them in Gadsden because, by the time they were born, Marvin was gone and three years later I'd moved to Birmingham to be near my two sons and their wives and families. My two daughters-in-law have been like real daughters to me and I am so grateful to have their love and support. This has made a difference in my life. Of course, Alfred and Robert are everything a Mother could want and I have such trust and love for them and from them.

Watching Philip and Abbey grow into two fine people has added joy to my life. We've shared some great times at "The Boathouse" and on trips where I have been included and I look forward to seeing them develop and mature into adulthood. They're on the brink now so that won't be long. Philip is growing into a special kind of independent person. In the past, I've enjoyed watching him "run like the wind" at his soccer games. Our loving relationship is deeply cherished and enjoyed.

Several weeks have passed since my last entry here. On February 16, 2002, Abbey celebrated her Bat Mitzvah. She was gloriously prepared and able and beautiful. She spoke well and remembered Marvin and Linda Gail in her remarks, as well as me, her grandmother. Robert made such a wonderful talk to Abbey from him and Eileen. They certainly gave us grandparents plenty of "kovid" (honor). Claire and I presented her Tallit and took part in passing the Torah "from generation to generation" and were also called for Alliyot. They gave all members of the family a part in the service. People came from 10 or more states and I got the bonus of having the grandchildren and grandnieces and nephews use my house for a gathering place when the festivities were over. My niece, Rosalie, and her family left for their home in Massachusetts on Tuesday morning.

How fortunate to have lived to enjoy four great-grandchildren: Joshua, Olivia, and Samuel Cohn, and John Speakes, IV. What blessings! The circumstances of Olivia's birth brought us many anxious moments. In December 2002, Marty's wife, Philippa, became very ill with a chest infection that was never really defined. Finally, a Cesarean section was performed and both Philippa and the baby were put on breathing machines. Philippa was so ill that she has no memory of what took place. Linda Shea left for England on December 25th and was in Reading to look after little Josh and support Marty. Michael flew over, too. I didn't know anything about the crisis until I returned from Sarasota on December 27th. By then little Olivia, weighing only 2 lbs. 6 oz. was in the special infant's care unit, and Philippa was beginning to slowly improve.

Today on February 10th as I write this, our little girl weighs 4 lbs. 4 oz. and is still in intensive care, but growing. May G__ grant her health and a normal existence. Philippa is home, but it will take six months to a year for her return to normal.

It is late February 2003, and we're all breathing a little easier now that our little Olivia weighs about 4 lbs. 12 oz and seems to be growing and developing. Philippa is much better, too. Linda is back home, and Marty and family are still planning to move to Gainesville, Florida where Marty has taken a position with the University of Florida. I am happy to report that in 2008 Olivia is thriving and has grown into a beautiful and appealing little girl.

Israel's 36th Birthday Party

In 1981 Marvin and I received an invitation from Alabama Governor Fob James and his wife to come to Montgomery, AL for a celebration of Israel's birthday. The party was to take place at the governor's mansion on Sunday afternoon, May 14th.

Of course, we were thrilled to learn of this happening in Alabama and accepted immediately. I have a copy of the program, but even without this reminder I think I remember every minute of this unusual event and will try to share it with you.

As we arrived at the governor's mansion, we were met and escorted by members of the Alabama Highway Patrol in full uniform. The mansion was decorated with Jewish ritual objects. A large Tallit was draped on a table with a Shofar and Menorah. As we entered the door we were greeted by a receiving line which included Mrs. James, the Israeli Consul from Atlanta, and a noted Evangelist among others. In the background Jewish and Hebrew musical selections were played by a violinist with piano accompaniment.

The table in the dining room was laden with kosher food – supervised by a Montgomery rabbi. After taking refreshment we were led out to the lovely grounds of the mansion. A large Star of David floated in the swimming pool. Chairs were arranged before a large platform where speakers and the Alabama Symphony Orchestra were scheduled for the program of celebration. Mrs. James presented a scroll and spoke of her love and devotion to the State of Israel and later she and the Governor cut the birthday cake. The Symphony played and the Israeli consul expressed his appreciation and that of his country. Hatikvah was sung as was the Star Spangled Banner. Rabbi Grafman of Temple Emanu-el gave the benediction. At the governor's mansion, we were certainly warmly welcomed and respected. All in all, it was a day in Alabama to remember.

De Gaulle once called Jews elitist and cosmopolitan. I think his point was that Jews couldn't be good "Frenchmen" like him or loyal citizens of any country. We all know that is false. But I'm not insulted. If we are "cosmopolitan," history has made us so. I for one love meeting Jews in every country I've ever visited and feeling a deep connection to each one.

We Travel to Russia

I don't think I've written anything about our trip to Russia to see our relatives. Izzy and I both wanted to make the trip and so did Marvin. Estelle decided not to go so our fourth traveling companion was Dr. Ed Miles. I had given a speech at the LJCC on our return and thought I still had a copy and could include it here. But I can't find it so will just tell you a little about this with the idea that if I can't remember something, it probably wasn't very important. It was the early 1980s and the communists were still in power. Russia wasn't anything like our free country which we took for granted, but we always had in the back of our minds that we didn't want to cause our relatives any harm. After talking it over, we did get visas and were required to name the people we expected to visit. In our baggage were clothes and whatever else we thought we would be allowed to bring our relatives. Upon arrival in Moscow, no one even looked into our luggage. On the bus from the airport to our hotel (The Russia, located right across the street from the Kremlin), I worried about how we would get in touch with our relatives and thought I hadn't made good enough plans. However, when we stepped off the bus at our hotel, which by the way was used only for foreign visitors, imagine our surprise when we heard someone call out, "Anya." To our delight, there were eleven members of our family to greet us. Our Russian relatives had made a long trip to Moscow to see us and planned to stay a few days at another hotel.

They were: my first cousin Sara (Mama's sister Slava's daughter), Sara's daughter Ina, Sara's sister, Anya, and her friend, cousin Ida and her daughter, Genya, (and Genya's husband and little girl), and Anya's son, Mareck, and his wife. Mareck is the only one who left Russia and went to Israel when emigration opened up for Jews.

We spent a lot of time with our family. Some of them spoke a little English and some of us spoke a little Yiddish. Intourist, our tour agency, was run by the government. But they did allow our relatives to accompany us one day when the bus took our group to the Space Museum. That night Mareck was our host at dinner at the hotel. It was very nice and mostly fish and other cold dishes. We had a wonderful visit, but when two well dressed men took a table near us, all conversation stopped. One day as we were visiting in our room, Ina kept dialing the telephone so our conversations couldn't be overheard as easily. A few months previous to this trip, Marvin and I had heard a lecture at Wild Acres, NC and we were told to assume our rooms were bugged.

Food was poor in Moscow, but after we got further into the country our meals improved. We did see some beautiful opera and ballet and even their famous circus. In Leningrad, we were enjoying a wonderful ballet when Izzy spotted someone he knew in the audience. It was David Vann, the Mayor of Birmingham, visiting along with some other southern mayors. Izzy called out his name and we met at intermission. We tried to visit the famous old synagogue in Leningrad and went there in a taxi, but found it closed.

We didn't get to visit Dnepropetrovsk, where our relatives lived, as foreigners were not allowed there. I did speak to my Aunt Slava over the phone. We had to use the facilities at the post office to make the call. Her voice was so like Mama's that I was moved to tears. But we did travel to the Ukraine and visited Kiev and Odessa and even Kharkov, which was located a short distance from Novozybkov, my parents' former home. I remember Papa talking about going to Kharkov on business as a young man when he had a hardware store. In Kiev we did go to Babi Yar and the men in our party said a Kaddish for those thousands buried there. The only overt anti-Semitism took place at two museums where they showed the same "original" painting. It depicted Jews stoning a young woman who had married a Christian.

When we got on our Pan American flight for home, they announced that the Russian Airlines would soon be taking over that route. I was delighted that we were now in the hands of our own people and on the way home. I still correspond with Sara regularly and she keeps me posted about the others. Aunt Slava is gone and Ina has married a second time. Genya's little Leona is now a grown woman. Both Sara and Anya have visited Mareck in Israel, but have expressed no desire to move there.

Other Travels

After our children were grown and had their own families, Marvin and I took many wonderful trips to Europe and to Israel. We once spent a whole month traveling in Europe and England. And we really did enjoy ourselves. I thought that if our marriage could withstand all that togetherness and sometimes not even speaking the local language, we'd never have to worry about getting along.

Many nice things happened to us while traveling abroad. Once, we were in London when we discovered that *Fiddler on the Roof* was playing there. I believe it was starring the fine Israeli actor Topol. We decided to attend the next night and took a taxi from our hotel to the theatre. Our taxi driver was a small, wiry man with sandy hair and a real cockney accent. Marvin always talked to our drivers and enjoyed the company of the local people. We got to the theatre in short order and as we were leaving the cab, this "cockney" called to us, "Zei Gezundt." That gave us a very warm feeling and it was the beginning of a great evening.

One spring, we were in Paris and decided to make a visit to the Loire River Valley and see the sights and the beautiful old castles there. At one stop we met a very nice couple. Marvin had offered to take a picture of them together. I thought they looked like two well-to-do burghers, maybe from Holland. Back on the bus as we were returning to Paris, this gentleman offered us some fruit and he began talking to Marvin. During the conversation he told Marvin that his wife didn't usually like to talk about it, but she was Geula Ben Gurian, daughter of David Ben Gurian, Israel's first Prime Minister and a world respected leader. The husband was General Emanuel Ben Eliezer. They gave us their home address and phone number and asked us to visit them on our next trip to Israel. But we never did get in touch with them. We had always felt lucky to live during the time that the State of Israel was established and to be able (though not living there or fighting in their army) to support Israel and to take some small part in helping our fellow Jews take refuge and settle in the Jewish homeland.

In 1983, we went on a trip to Europe with the Rubin Brothers Company and then stopped in England. There, Marvin and I decided to stay another week or two and to rent a car. Marvin was brave about driving in England and we visited north of London – to Stratford-on-Avon, to Oxford, to the beautiful home and estate of Sir Winston Churchill, and more. Then we drove through the Cotswold's where we stopped at one of their "jumble sales" at a local church. We drove into Bath in the late afternoon and while looking for a hotel, discovered that we could join a local sightseeing tour right then.

We joined the group, and never did make it to the hotel. That afternoon I stepped in a pothole and broke my femur. We found out that Britain's state medical facilities were very good. My surgery was successful (I still have the hardware in my leg), and the care was more than good.

Marvin still didn't have a place to stay. He finally did find a nice little hotel, but could only have his room for three days as the hotel was already fully booked after that. So Marvin was left looking for new quarters. One day he came to my room and brought a beautiful young woman with him. Her name was Gina. She wore her dark hair in bangs and was just a "knock-out." Gina worked at the hospital as some kind of photographer. Well, Gina was trying to help Marvin with finding a place. The next day, he came to see me – lying in bed after surgery, pale and looking pretty awful. Then he told me, "Gina has just been divorced and she told me that I could stay at her apartment. I think the ex-husband lives next door." My answer came quickly – even in my weakened condition – "**Uh uh!** I may be down, but I'm not out!" We had a good laugh! Alfred and Robert arrived in Bath within the next few days and they all found suitable housing. By sheer coincidence, Martha and John Speaks were visiting in England at that time too, and they came to Bath to see us as well.

Before leaving Bath, just thirteen days after the surgery, I was able to go up and down a full flight of stairs on crutches. On the flight home, I was not allowed to sit up on the plane, but the airline had given us four seats so we'd have room for a cot. All I can remember about that trip was that they forgot to send along a bed pan (we made one out of a little basket) and that the captain of the plane kept sending me messages and asking me how I was getting along. We flew directly to Atlanta and came on home by ambulance. The downstairs of our house was my place of recovery. There was plenty of room to get around and, also, to receive company. The food was brought down or sent on the dumb waiter and the care was excellent. After a while, I was back to normal and surrounded by my loving family, but I do believe the shock of this accident took a toll on my fine husband.

Another time, Marvin and I took a month long trip up the east coast and had a wonderful time exploring and visiting with friends we knew along the way. When we got to Columbia, Pennsylvania where

Joel Sater and his wife Denise lived, Joel greeted us with much affection and warmth. At the time, he was publishing a newspaper for antique dealers. (It was widely distributed even here in Alabama.) Marvin and Joel had grown up together in Birmingham and had great memories and good laughs to share. Joel and Denise had made up our bed with red satin sheets which were so slippery that I almost slid out of our high bed. He was a victim of cancer, too, and died about a year before Marvin. But on that trip we enjoyed the beautiful fall foliage and discovered interesting places. We even stopped to see Abe Quellman and Anita on Long Island. That was a carefree trip as we had no hard and fast plans, but just looked up places in our *AAA Tour Book* and stopped where we pleased. We even went up into the Catskills and went by to see Ethel's family, the Greens, in Middletown. They were very gracious and spoke of Ethel very fondly and with high regard.

We went on to Saratoga, NY, took the baths, and went to the races. It really was a wonderful time. I just wish Marvin was here to add his impressions to mine. He really did enjoy Maine, New Hampshire and all the rest. Going by car was a good choice for this member of the "automobile generation" who never tired of driving.

When I lost Marvin I was sure that was the end of my traveling experiences. However, that was a wrong assumption. When Marty phoned me sometime in 1988 to ask if I'd like to go to Israel with him, I thought that was the nicest invitation I'd had in a long time. And we did go and had a wonderful trip. Those kinds of things don't happen very often in a lifetime.

I Lose Marvin

Throughout his life, Marvin had undergone several surgeries. As a boy, he had an appendectomy. Later on, he had a thyroidectomy and then a serious surgery for diverticulitis. His back gave him trouble for years because of herniated disks, but that left him when he lost weight. In 1984-85 Marvin seemed to be fine. He had lost weight after his colon surgery. He had cut down on his work hours and we were traveling and enjoying our family and friends. Alfred and Robert had taken over much of Marvin's responsibilities in the business.

Alfred and Linda were enjoying a growing family with 3 fine boys. Linda and John and family were happy in Atlanta. Robert had finally broken with Jackie and that unhappy relationship and was getting ready to marry Eileen. In fact, we were down at Destin at our time-share apartment at Seascape with Grace and Syd Finkel when Marvin began to complain about a strange irritated feeling around his esophagus. He didn't know what the trouble was, but didn't think it significant. He did go to a walk-in clinic in Destin where he was given some kind of medicine to relieve the symptoms.

On our return home, Dr. Bill Ennis, who had helped treat Marvin for diverticulitis, must have suspected something more serious because he put Marvin in the hospital. He was soon in isolation to protect him as there were signs of a blood condition. Dr. Ennis encouraged us to go to UAB for further studies as Marvin showed symptoms of leukemia. I was especially frightened by the prospect of this diagnosis because my sister, Sarah, had lost her life from that disease.

We drove into Birmingham as soon as Dr. Ennis had made an appointment for us. It was the next day, I think. At the UAB clinic we noticed so many sick looking people while Marvin looked hale and hearty. I was sure the lab had made a mistake in diagnosis. When we met with Dr. Barton, a hematologist who was assigned to us, he was unhesitating in his prognosis – pre-myelogenous leukemia – and Marvin would have less than a year to live.

This doctor gave us no hope to carry us through and hearing that death sentence hit us like a bolt of lightning. We felt this man had no feelings for his patients and asked for another doctor. We were then placed under the care of the Dean of the Medical School, Dr. Charles Scott, a little older and a lot kinder. Marvin elected not to take the strongest treatment as we were told it wouldn't do any good as far as a cure was concerned. However, we did go to Birmingham regularly for some treatment and even took an apartment at Park Towers for several months to be near the hospital in case of emergency.

Doctors in the Hematology Department took turns seeing patients at UAB hospital, and Dr. Barton (our initial contact) saw Marvin when he was on rotation. He really did try to be kind and to get friendly with Marvin. (We had been generous to a young boy who was one of his patients and I guess the doctor knew about it.) As fate would have it, Dr. Barton was on rotation when the end came. Marvin was fully aware of everything and brave and a wonderful man to the end. I, on the other hand, have felt since that day that I didn't talk to him enough, and while Robert and I were with him, I should have given him more assurance as to how we all felt about him. Guess I must have thought he already knew all that, but now I know it's good to hear someone say, "I love you," and mean it. So the regret stays with me.

Marvin certainly left his mark on our world not only for his beloved and loving family, but also for scores of people he had contact with through his business life, as well as through his civic, charitable, and religious work. People were drawn to him because of his kindness and personality and friendliness and consideration. Marvin was completely non-judgmental. What an endearing trait. I do believe that was one of the reasons people were drawn to him.

Marvin Phillip Cohn was, and is still, a force to be remembered with love and respect by those who knew him personally and those who knew him only by reputation. Like his beautiful and gallant mother who was widowed at age 33 and left with two sons, then 13 and 8 years old, he always faced life with courage, optimism, common sense, and goodwill.

In November 2002, sixteen years after his death, Marvin was honored posthumously in Gadsden by the Etowah Patriot Association and inducted into the Patriots Hall of Honor. I was escorted to a seat on the stage and accepted the plaque for him and for our family. Our old friend Colonel Andy Chaffin had placed his name in nomination I find it remarkable and significant that he was still remembered so well and strongly even 16 years after his death. Prior to his death, Marvin had been honored by the Alltrusa Club as "Citizen of the Year" and he was memorialized with his portrait being hung in the Gadsden City Hall. The Etowah County Red Cross also named an award for him in honor of his past work and contribution to the success of that group.

During his lifetime, Marvin was loved and honored and appreciated, too, as a leader and humanitarian. How blessed I was to have him as my husband and soul mate and best friend.

Continuance

After such a marriage and such a husband, how can one go on? I often wonder about that and about myself. Here's what did happen. Marcia Harris Sacks had been diagnosed with breast cancer in 1989. She and Jay came to UAB Hospital for a second opinion. Sadly, this turned out to be the same as the first. On a Sunday I came to Birmingham to see them at the hospital. Going back to my car, I crossed the street in the middle of the block and was hit by a speeding pick-up truck. This resulted in the fracture of my knee that left me recovering at the Robert Cohn's for a number of weeks (like "The Man Who Came to Dinner"). Leonard Lewis and I had already begun to spend time together. He was very attentive now and began to take me out to dine as soon as I had improved enough to use crutches.

As all this was going on, I realized I really should live closer to my sons and decided to move back to Birmingham. Leonard helped me find a place to live and even assisted in organizing and packing for the move to Carriage Place in November, 1989. I had known Leonard and his late wife Pearl for a long time. We were from the same background and shared many of the same interests. When I went to Sarasota for the winter months, he followed me there. His family and friends embraced and welcomed me. This relationship lasted for about seven years before it ended.

I had moved back to Birmingham by this time and was renewing old friendships as well as making some new friends. The activities in the Jewish Community and the cultural life offered in Birmingham were filling my time nicely. All this came to a halt when a scheduled mammogram revealed a small tumor in my left breast. It was cancerous. A lumpectomy was performed, followed by some weeks of radiation. My luck was still holding and ten years later I still seem to be free of the disease.

A short time later, Arnold Royal came into my life. He was still practicing pediatrics part time and was full of energy and life. He had been a gifted and beloved doctor. Arnold and I had been in the same Confirmation Class at Beth-El and, also, I had been very fond of his late wife Elaine, a fine person and respected leader in the Jewish community. Guess I never did have any kind of relationship with anyone I hadn't known forever. We both loved Israel and had a lot of interests in common. And both of us loved dancing. Arnold had a very large circle of friends who readily accepted me, as did his family. All this enlarged my life and daily experience. It was a shame that he had some serious health problems and suffered much illness before his death in November 2002. His family had taken me in as theirs and I, especially, gained a little sister and brother with Micky and Stanley Rubenstein. My good friends Ophelia and David Massey were very fond of Arnold and we enjoyed a very pleasant social life together. When I moved to Carriage Place, David and Ophelia were my new neighbors and they "took me under their wings" and helped me resettle in Birmingham. David and Arnold had known each other as boys, and David and I had attended Ramsay in the same class. Now David is gone too, but I still cherish my ties to Ophelia.

Tragedy struck again in November 2002. During the middle of that month, we learned that Alan and Charlotte Cohn lost their son, Lawrence. He had been suffering from depression, but no one suspected that he would end his own life. He left a beautiful little daughter named Mollie and his estranged wife. Charlotte and Alan were devastated, of course. Since our families have not been on the best of terms for several years, this loss was very hard on all...especially Linda S. and Alfred. We all went to Gadsden to express our sorrow and support and to try to express our sympathy. I, especially, feel so sad about our family break because we were unusually close for such a long time. I'm afraid we'll never be able to return to our relationship of those earlier days.

I Lose Linda Gail

Linda Gail became ill in September, 1988, and she died in January, 1997 after nine years of fighting ovarian cancer. At first we were told that her prognosis was good because the trouble was found early. That, however, was not the case. When discovered, the cancer had already begun to spread. She did have better times and she was brave and intelligent and knowledgeable with her treatments. She even went back to college and got a second graduate degree, this time in Library Science. She was able to hold a position as librarian at DeKalb County College and enjoyed it and the young students there. She was a very understanding and good wife and mother. My own relationship with Linda leaves me with regret. For some reason I couldn't be more completely open and show more understanding. I was kept at arms length and never knew exactly why. When she was younger, before her marriage, we were very close and I always felt she was the perfect daughter. Materially, we were always generous. Maybe that had something to do with it. She didn't seem to try to influence John and Jacob in our relationship, as we always were and are still very close and loving.

At a memorial service held for Linda Gail in Atlanta several months after her death, I met my daughter in a new light and learned how loved and respected she was by her many women friends. She was a very special person, honest and kind and completely unselfish. In July, 2005 Linda's husband, John Jr., took me by the college library to see their memorial to Linda. We met other library workers and I could see how loved and liked and respected she was.

Still, I remember with pleasure her laugh and happy giggle along with her serious ideas and interests. She was a completely "civilized" person, intellectual on a level many do not attain. This is a little thing, I guess, but she bought gifts carefully (with her limited funds) and I can just see her bringing to others lovely and thoughtful treasures. And her dear children bring me such pleasure, especially now when I need them. John Jr. remains close to our family. We haven't yet talked about Linda Gail, and I suspect the wounds are still too raw for both of us.

Right now, just a few days after Linda Gail's Yarzite, five years since we lost her, she is ever in my mind and heart and I don't even have to close my eyes to see her and feel her presence. Marvin, too, has been gone for 15 years already but he is welded into my being. How lucky I've been to share my life with such a good and fine person, strong and noble. My memory is full of beloved and close family members who are now gone. I've found that people can be very resilient and strong in spite of tragedy, because after losing Marvin and then Linda Gail, and so many other loved ones, I just keep on going. How can that be?

Life Goes On

Today is January 10, 2003. I haven't written anything for many weeks now because the present has become too painful. Sorrows of the past have risen to the top of my consciousness. Memory isn't always selective or even compassionate. Everything comes back whether willed or not. Arnold's death brought back so many sad memories and lent to my living those times over and over. I really felt physically and mentally weak for some time and achingly wrapped in sorrow. But people really are stronger than one would imagine. Last night Robert took me to the Alabama Symphony concert featuring a wonderful young violinist. He was Israeli, I think. I enjoyed the concert very much and Robert and I had a good time laughing and just plain enjoying ourselves and life.

My grandson, Michael, will be in Birmingham tomorrow and I'm looking forward to our spending some time together. Dan just phoned me out of the blue. He couldn't have called at a better time as I've been feeling a bit "down" and tired. But, thank G__ my health is holding up and I'm feeling quite independent.

I don't know how we continue after so much heartache, but somehow we find a way to go on. I remain very active, even though I'm in my eighties. I am surrounded by the people I love, and I keep my mind busy. I even continue to travel quite a bit, and I have seen things that I never would have imagined. A few years ago Grace and I took a cruise on the Mediterranean Sea and stopped at Ephesus in Turkey. Our guide was a lovely dark haired beauty and her English was perfect. At one point she told us that they had recently found a carving of an etrog and a lulav on one of the ruined buildings. We could see very well the Menorah on the old library wall. Well, I thought it strange that anyone not Jewish would know about the etrog and lulav so I asked her and found out she was Jewish and lived in a town south of Ephesus. I felt such a bond with this young woman and I think she did too. She introduced me to her sister (also a guide). When we parted we hugged and wished each other many Shaloms. Being Jewish seems to add a very special dimension to travel.

On Mother's Day 2004, Alfred took me, along with Linda Shea and his whole family, to West Palm Beach, Florida. We all stayed at the Ritz Carlton Hotel and had a wonderful time together. I've painted the white and red roses he gave me on Mother's Day. The gift of being with Marty, Philippa, Josh, Olivia and Michael and Dan filled my heart with great joy. How lovely to be part of that family and to feel so cherished by my fine son. He's a lot like his father.

Just this year in 2005, Howard Sarasohn called me and asked if I'd like to go to Venezuela with him. My answer was prompt and a big "yes." A few years ago Venezuela would have been the last place I'd choose to visit. But at this time John III and his family were in Caracas and that included my newest great-grandchild, John IV. John and Susan's child Morgan has developed into a cherished great-granddaughter too – very much loved by all.

John is in the Foreign Service of the U.S. State Department. So Howard and I had lots of telephone conversations about our travel plans and I met him at the Atlanta Airport on April 8th to begin our trip. He is a very nice and pleasant traveling companion and I think we both enjoyed each other's company. Besides, Howard was knowledgeable and considerate and we really had a good time.

We arrived on a weekend so John was able to spend that time with us. Susan and Morgan and both Johns were a great pleasure – especially since the Speaks knew Spanish and we didn't. We did sight-seeing in Caracas and got the flavor of the city. On Monday morning, Howard and I flew over to the old colonial city of Coro. While there we visited the old city and the Peninsula. But the most interesting part to me was finding an old Synagogue (now in a museum) from the 1800's and the oldest Jewish Cemetery in South America. On our return to Caracas on Thursday, we had wonderful visits with the family and more interesting forays into "historical Caracas" and into the countryside. After our return trip to the Atlanta airport, Howard saw that I was taken care of and left me to take the Airport Express back to Birmingham while he flew on to California.

Just about a month later, we met again in Amherst at Jonathon Eisen's Bar Mitzvah. That was a lovely time, too. All Rosalie's and Ephraim's family were there and Jonathon did us all proud. There were eight or nine rabbis at the service on Saturday, and it was a glorious celebration for all the family and guests who took part in the service. I was given the honor of presenting Jonathon with his Bar Mitzvah tallit. I'm sure everyone felt as surrounded by love as I did. The celebration lasted a little longer for me as I stayed a few extra days and reaped such "naches" being in the Eisen household and feeling so welcome.

On returning home from Amherst in March, 2006, I found Alfred in the hospital. He had been diagnosed with lymphoma. My dear first born had never even been in the hospital since his birth so this illness came as a complete shock to us all. He has under gone over two years of powerful treatment and a number of side effects and set backs. The year 2008 finds him still using all his intellect and strength to overcome the disease. Of course, Linda Shae and their three fine sons have been by his side every step of the way with concern, love and support. Now in January, 2008, we are all praying for recovery and a return to the happy and productive life he deserves. For a mother who has already seen too much of illness in loved ones, there is always apprehension along with never-ending hope. Happily, in February the birth of Alfred and Linda's grandson, Samuel Thomas Cohn, brought joy to the family. I do think Alfred is feeling better today and stronger and looking to the future. And I know he'll soon be his old energetic and active person. All his life he has been such a joy to me and Marvin, too. I've always been proud of his fine character and high spirits.

I've been blessed, too with very warm nieces and nephews. Eddy Harris and his family and I became closer than ever on my stays in Sarasota. Rosalie Harris-Eisen has become like a daughter. Her mother, my sister Pauline, was very important to me all my life and now Rosalie is filling that space. Because of her, I've gotten to know parts of the U.S. that otherwise would have been strange to me. When he lived,

Marvin, too, loved visiting Rosalie in Oregon and California. During the past few years, I've grown very fond of New England and sharing some of the Eisen's busy lives. (Jacob and Jennifer are now making their home in New England, too, and that brings it all that much closer to my life.)

Family has been my strongest attachment in life but not my only source of happiness. Good friends have been and are still very important to daily living. So I'd be remiss in not sharing my appreciation of that particular blessing here. There are too many to be listed on this page and I know I'll probably leave out some who are very dear to me. In spite of this, I must mention just a few.

Grace Finkel has been my dear and loyal friend for many years. It is so wonderful to be at ease and able to discuss frankly just about anything with her at anytime. Micky Rubenstein has come into my life in these later years. I know how lucky I am to have her and Stanley's uncompromising companionship and friendship and even love. Blanche Rogoff and I still remain in close touch. My good friends Ethel Laufman and Betty Anfanger are also my Mah Jong buddies. All my good friends enrich my life every day.

Rachel Polhill could have a whole chapter in this book. We have not been life-long friends but it seems to me that we have. She has been good company and generous with her time and talent. She probably has never given all this a thought and doesn't realize how she is admired by others.

Conclusion

So what do I leave my descendents? If I had a direct line to G__, I'd ask Him for compassion and blessings for all His people. I tremble a little when I wonder about their world because I know what people are capable of doing. Still, I hope theirs will be the "One World" we're hearing about. And I really do feel that the Jewish people will continue to thrive and be an influence for good in it. Surely, our long existence in history must be part of some design that fosters a profound purpose and plan.

Reflections

A local department store in Birmingham was innovative for the times. During the 1920's and 1930's they were doing promotions to improve customer relations. Saturday morning programs were presented for children. I remember one vividly and have never seen anything like it since.

On an upstairs floor of the building, actors presented well-known fairy tales or stories. The one that comes to mind now may have been Cinderella. The unusual part was this: the live actors performed behind a glass screen that minimized their size. They appeared to be tiny people, perfect in every way, but just tiny. This was a wonderful sight that delighted the small children. Because of their size, we children didn't find the stories overwhelming or the villains threatening. They were just the right size for us. We could even hold them in our hands if we so desired. All this comes back so many years later.

Sometimes I wonder if my memory might be using that same kind of screen. Otherwise, how could all those special people crowd into my head? There's no doubt about it. They come into view often. The images, though small, are very clear. I see these dear ones as they were physically and also their characters and personalities. Usually there isn't any action involved- maybe just a smile or nod. Still, there's a feeling of strong presence. What dear company! My first act should be to invite them all out from behind the "glass screen" and to introduce them to others who will care and enjoy renewing relationships and memories. Some part of them will surely be understood and cherished. Now to begin…

Vignettes

Papa

Papa (1880-1955)

Jacob Euchvitz leaned against the rail of the *SS Pallanza* and looked at the sea with un-seeing eyes. He seemed to be quite alone ever since embarking at Hamburg, Germany. However, if it were possible to look into this young man's mind and heart, one might find a host of people inhabiting his detailed memories of the past. Strange, because this voyage was supposed to be the source of new plans and hopes for the future.

In spite of himself, Jacob's mind turned back to his boyhood in the Ukraine and the sorrow of a six-year old lad losing his father. So almost as far back as he could remember, Jacob's mother had been the head of the family and also, its provider. From her small store on the grounds of the local match factory, his mother tended her children and kept her family together. It wasn't an easy life but they were not an unhappy group. The children received the education available and good moral values to guide them in later life. Jacob's natural, pleasant personality and dauntless spirit was still evident. He thought of his youth with pleasure and smiled inwardly remembering "rescuing" Dasche Malkin after she had fallen in the local river. Was it true that you must always take care of someone whose life you had saved? When would he see her again?

This voyage was not the first adventure for Jacob. He had traveled many hundreds of miles after the Russo-Japanese War around 1904-5. Only in his twenties then, Jacob boarded the Trans-Siberian Railway for a long journey to Harbin, Manchuria with hopes of seeking his fortune there. Thinking of those days, Jacob looked at the split finger nail on his right hand and remembered the time he had defended himself and his belongings from an unsavory Chinese fellow in Harbin. Still, he was making his way toward some success when word reached Jacob of the pogroms in Russia and the Ukraine. Jewish people were suffering and in danger. His heart sank when he thought of his widowed mother and his younger sister. They needed him and he would return home at once.

And now, several years later, here Jacob was again traveling to another far-off land, still looking for a better life. This time, his destination was the U.S.A. The Statue of Liberty would soon be in view. On leaving Novozybkov, Jacob had left most of his money with his mother and also, some to be used as a dowry for his sister. After all, everyone said that in America "the streets were paved with gold" so making a living in the U.S would be no problem. The ship soon docked and Jacob was pushed out of his reverie and forced to take a good square look at the present.

Jobs were available. However, Jacob's free spirit and optimistic nature were sorely tried when he was hired by the Waltham Clock Company near New York City. The company actually locked up their immigrant workers at night so they would be ready for work in the morning. This didn't appeal to Jacob. He soon decided that if these were the conditions in a "free country," he'd return to his home and family in Russia as soon as possible.

Luckily for all the Euchvitz children, Dasche Malkin arrived on the scene just at this time. The brave young couple decided to face the future together as man and wife. They settled in Birmingham, Alabama where a relative already resided and they wouldn't feel alone and far from family. The climate in Alabama was a lot like the Ukraine and the small town life suited them too. Destiny sometimes leads us on circuitous routes to our special fate. This young man's traveling days were over. His time and energy were now directed toward caring for and supporting his wife and, in time, four children. Jacob accepted his life with grace, was much loved and remains a special force for good in those who remember him so well.

Mama

Mama (1882 – 1974)

The *SS Kroonland* left Antwerp, Belgium in early January, 1907 bound for the United States. The steerage deck was crowded with Europeans immigrating to the "Golden Medina," the United States. Dasche Malkin was one of these passengers.

Dasche was filled with mixed feelings of expectation and anxiety on taking this big step in changing her previous life. She was twenty-five years old, but her adventures into the world outside her little shtetl had, so far, been experienced only in books. Besides, she missed the company of her dear parents and her six sisters. Her only brother was traveling to America, too. However, he was on another deck, traveling in first class.

To say the conditions were overcrowded was an understatement. The trip from her home in Novozybkov to Antwerp had been long and arduous, but she was finally boarded and on her way to the United States. Soon, Dasche would be in New York and under the care of her mother's brother, Uncle Katz. Thoughts of her good uncle filled our traveler with warmth and comfort.

The Kroonland was a large steamship. It held

1537 passengers in first class, and about a thousand in second-class. There were many more in steerage, but an accurate count was never established. According to historians, steerage was not a deck, but a section between decks which was formerly used for storage-sometimes carrying "steers." With mass emigration from Eastern Europe, this space was now converted into living quarters for passengers. Temporary partitions had been installed for these poor travelers. Meals were plain and served without regard to basic etiquette.

The Kroonland's passengers were predominately from Hungary and Eastern Europe. Dasche spoke neither English nor Hungarian. She was proficient in Russian and also in Yiddish, that international language that had served a scattered people for many years. Conversing with other people mitigated the loneliness, fear, and helplessness in Dasche's deepest being. Dasche kept telling herself that life on the Kroonland was a temporary condition. Soon she would be in New York and in the midst of family.

The ship's twin engines could travel at a speed of seventeen knots. Every minute was bringing Dasche closer to her destination. She tried to be patient, and soon she met a nice woman, as well as a sweet family with children. When it came time for meals, Dasche strictly kept the laws of Kashrut and was prepared for a limited diet. However, she was not prepared for winter in the middle of the Atlantic Ocean.

A storm developed and high waves tossed the giant Kroonland around as if it were a small craft. It was impossible to stand upright. Dasche took to her bunk with violent seasickness. What misery! She was much too nauseated to take any food and became weaker and more despondent by the day. Eventually, a ship's doctor or attendant entered her quarters to check on her. He tried repeatedly to get her to take food, but each time she refused. Finally, in desperation, he told her, "If you don't take some kind of nourishment soon, we'll have to throw you overboard." With that threat, she allowed him to spoon feed her a bit of gruel and he made it his business to see that she received the necessary attention.

Eventually, conditions improved and the weather began to calm. The remainder of the journey was tiring, but not impossible to manage. Then, on a morning that seemed like any other, excitement filled the ship as the Kroonland steamed into New York Harbor and everyone rushed to see the welcoming torch of the Statue of Liberty.

On landing at Ellis Island, Dasche's brother was immediately taken into the country. Steerage passengers had to stay on Ellis Island to be cleared for entrance. There were examinations, questions, record taking, and various other forms of "red tape." Dasche began to feel completely abandoned. She was in an unfamiliar land with no knowledge of the language or what to expect, but she got through the ordeal and one afternoon was delivered into the care of Uncle Katz.

On arriving at her uncle's home in New York City, Dasche was greeted with great kindness by her family. Another person was waiting for her, too, someone very handsome and important to Dasche. There stood Jacob Euchvitz from Novozybkov with arms outstretched and welcoming. He was as loving as ever and so happy to be with his sweetheart again that he told her he would cancel his plans to return to Russia if Dasche would consent to become his wife.

Since none of this immigrant group cared for the crowded conditions and atmosphere of New York, they decided to leave for another place where they had some close relatives. Rabbi Leibovitz led the Knesseth Israel synagogue in Birmingham, Alabama. Mrs. Leibovitz was related to Dasche, and these good people encouraged the newcomers to come down to Birmingham. And that's how the four Euchvitz children got to be Southerners.

After marrying in Birmingham, Dasche and Jacob lived out their lives as good American citizens, adjusting to their new land and language. As soon as they could afford to do so, they brought over Dasche's sister Hannah and also, Jacob's sister Rose and her family. Jacob never spoke much about the "Old Country," but Dasche always longed for her far-off family and the Russian culture she had left behind so many years before. No one knows if she would have changed her history had it been possible. She died at the age of ninety- three in Gadsden, Alabama . . . still a stranger in a strange land.

Pauline with husband Sam Harris

Pauline (1908 – 1975)

Pauline was the oldest child in the Euchvitz family of three daughters and one son. The psychologists tell us that the oldest child is usually the most aggressive and ambitious in many ways. That assessment didn't hold true in Pauline's case. She was the kindest, gentlest and most considerate of all the family (maybe not counting Papa). Her lovely large brown eyes reflected her sweet spirit and gentility.

Soon after completing her school years, Pauline went to work as an office manager, a very responsible position in a local wholesale jobbing company. Because that business extended credit to small merchants around the state, it held a very important and necessary place in the economy of those times. In fact, many of these small merchants couldn't have existed without the friendly and accommodating jobbers. The Great Depression was still holding sway. Pauline's position was critical to her company and its customers, too, as she was in charge of the credit records.

Even though times were hard, workers still earned vacation time. One summer Pauline spent her vacation time in New Orleans with her friends, the Brenner girls. All these young women were active in a young Zionists group called Junior Hadassah. That was how they met, through their work for the people who were building up Palestine as a haven and a Jewish homeland. The Brenners, an old and respected family in New Orleans, were leaders in the Jewish community as well. So it seems a little strange that one of their best friends was a young Christian professor at a local Catholic university. His name was James and he and Pauline really "hit it off."

James and Pauline spent many happy times together during those summer days in New Orleans. On her return home, it became evident to her parents that this had been a special "meeting," for the very next week Pauline received a package from James. The package contained a beautifully crafted scrap book with clever references to their time together in New Orleans. There were pictures, poems and private quotes understood only by the two of them. Pauline's reaction to the gift remained private. Whether or not her response was warm isn't known. Her beautiful dark eyes seemed softer as she quietly considered this turn of events in her life.

It isn't known whether Pauline's parents expressed their own reaction to what they considered a problem. To them being Jewish was of prime importance in life. After all, before coming to the

United States of America they had borne the repressive rules for Jews in Czarist Russia and suffered pogroms and general anti-Semitism. They knew well the history of their people and their world. Might they have unconsciously passed on some of this uneasiness and discomfort to their children? There is no doubt that Pauline felt a deeply rooted responsibility to her loved ones. She might have been torn between her feelings for this new friend and her loyalty to her family.

Surely, Pauline wrote James a nice letter of thanks, but was she rather non-committal? The following week another package arrived for Pauline from James. This one contained two leather bound copies of *Elbert Hubbard's Scrap Book*, a beautifully edited collection of excerpts from the best literature. As one might expect, the author had included romantic love pieces and works of deep meaning and feeling. These books made their way to the family book shelves and there they remained.

How Pauline responded to this last gift stayed locked in her tender heart and was never discussed. The next summer the Brenner girls and their brother came to Birmingham to visit. James never appeared.

Later, Pauline married Sam Harris and became the mother of four fine children, two daughters and two sons, who were all a blessing to her. Yet, one wonders how many times in life we are offered the chance to meet our Soul Mate… Did Pauline ever get that chance again?

Sarah with husband Jake Sarasohn

Sarah (1910 – 1953)

It should probably be pretty easy to get Sarah out from behind our glass screen. But, how can anyone ever get her down on a written page? That would be like trying to hold a glistening dew drop in your hand. Her beautiful, smiling face was just the surface picture of her energy and attractive, many faceted personality.

For instance, she was very good at sports. She played basketball for the "Y" and was also a beautiful swimmer. Yet, she was the only one in the family who could sew on Mama's Singer Sewing Machine and stitched up just about anything she wished. Her friends always loved her even though she tended to speak her mind and favored "the truth" to compromise. These relationships were tempered by Sarah's complete honesty and willingness to give a helping hand where needed.

As a young woman, already holding a job, Sarah and her friend Jake opened a joint savings account at their bank. No one else knew about this arrangement. They were trying to accumulate enough money to make a trip to Palestine. His parents were from Jerusalem and still owned some property there. This plan became known when the young people decided to get married instead. Jake and his "Mrs. Darling" set out to make a life together. And they did. At first they rented a small apartment, then a larger one. At one time they found it necessary to move back home with Sarah's family where they all pooled resources during hard times.

After that, they built their own house. The lot they had selected was then thought to be way out of town. Today the location is right in the middle of Mountain Brook, off Montevallo Road. Their home on Overbrook Road, not yet paved, faced empty fields where Jake cultivated a large vegetable garden.

Like everyone else, World War II affected all their plans. Even men with families were being drafted for military service. Jake joined the navy. Sarah and Jake took their little daughter and son and left their comfortable home for the U.S. Navel Base in Pensacola, Florida, where they luckily spent the war years. On their return, this young family sold their home in Mountain Brook, bought a small business in Bessemer, Alabama and resumed their efforts in home making and rearing their two children. They were making new friends and a place for themselves.

It came as a complete surprise and blow, out of the blue, for illness to strike this dynamic, young woman. However, that is what came into their lives next. Our beautiful, free spirited and shimmering "dew drop" was too quickly gathered into the arms of a higher power. She was only 43 years old.

Behind the glass screen and in the hearts of those who loved her, Sarah is still shining brightly. Somehow that doesn't really quiet the ever present feeling of loss.

Isadore with wife Estelle (Eisenberg)

Isadore (1913 - 1994)

Iz was part of the "Greatest Generation." Also, he was what is called a self-made man. That sort of person is difficult to keep behind my "glass screen." He is always escaping and appearing again even bigger than life.

As to being part of the "Greatest Generation," Iz did serve in the U.S. infantry during World War II and took part in famous and important battles in France and Germany. When the war was over, he returned a medaled, twice wounded Captain. It seems to me that his history merits the name self-made, too.

His business, The Boutique Bootery and Bazaar, was highly successful. He didn't inherit his start, but made it on his own with the help of his dear and devoted wife, Estelle. They were both very attractive and she was stunning and stylish. Besides, they knew the world of fashion and worked hard to make a go of it. I call that self-made, too.

Iz was the only son in a close and warm family that also included his three sisters. He was adored by his mother and the pride of his father and really loved and enjoyed by his sisters. He was six years older than his youngest sister and always present in her life and inside her "glass screen."

As a young boy he seemed to be always wearing out the knees of his knickers playing marbles. He cherished his "aggies" and sometimes allowed his little sister to handle them. There wasn't much organized play in our neighborhood. The children were forced to use their imaginations and invent their own games. For instance, they hand made their own wooden guns that fired off rubber bands cut from old inner tubes. With this ammunition they played war and cowboys and Indians. Once, his best playmates from across the street actually built a wooden roller coaster that started in their front yard and ended up under their house. As a small boy his best friend was a little African-American boy named Snowball. Snowball lived in the alley in back of Iz's house.

Iz's Bar Mitzvah was a time for great celebration. Papa and Mama invited all their friends to our house on Sunday for a big party. Mama had been preparing food for weeks before. On the Saturday of the Bar Mitzvah service at Knesseth Israel Synagogue, a luncheon was served and all the children were given bags of candy to commemorate this sweet day.

As he began developing into manhood, Iz became tall and good looking. His friendly personality and sense of humor surfaced and also, his athletic ability. Along with the other children in the family, Iz was given music lessons. He became accomplished on the clarinet. At Phillips High School, he cut quite a figure as Drum Major of the band. John Phillip Sousa, the great composer and leader of the U.S. Military Band, came to Birmingham and took time to conduct the Phillips High School band. So Iz could always laugh and tell people he had played under the direction of Sousa. I remember loving all those marches, too, and never hear *Stripes and Stripes Forever* or the *American Patrol March* without seeing Iz standing in front of our radio directing some unseen band.

Iz and Estelle were married before he went overseas during World War II. They later reared three lovely daughters Linda, Susan and Judi. The youngest, Judi, was planning her wedding to Bobby Webber when Iz was stricken with a serious illness. This resulted in a thirteen-hour operation and the necessity of wearing an artificial health-aid. These were dangerous days, but he did recover and accepted his situation with good grace. He remained a dapper dresser and now spent much time helping others learn to manage similar physical disabilities. Iz did make it to his youngest daughter's wedding and gave her away in style.

His warmth and sense of humor endeared Iz to many who knew him as boy and man. Bringing a bit of joy to others is no small thing in this world of ours and should be added to the accomplishments of our self-made man and member of the "Greatest Generation."

Somewhat True Stories

A Happy Mistake

This all happened at our local Temple. It's considered a small branch of that Celestial organization – exact address unknown. Of course, branches can't communicate with the main office by mail, wire or fax, but there are other methods of sending messages even though there's rarely any receipt of actual delivery. However, this method has been used for hundreds of years even though it does involve some bit of spiritual faith.

On the day our story took place, the Temple Sisterhood was sponsoring a luncheon to be followed by Mah Jong. Funds raised were dedicated to a local charity. So there were quite a number of women in attendance, having a good time and feeling quite righteous about writing their checks to a worthy cause.

For some reason my good friend and Mah Jong buddy didn't feel quite up to par that afternoon. She did eat some of the lunch and took her place at the Mah Jong table. Suddenly, she began to feel quite dizzy. Trying to concentrate on the Mah Jong tiles as a way to fight off this queer feeling, she finally lost control and fainted dead away - completely unable to function. Of course, this caused much excitement among the ladies. One friend, a former nurse, took charge. Her tender ministrations did help. In a short while the Emergency Medics arrived, did their examination and strongly advised taking the patient to the hospital Emergency Room That didn't work because the patient (having had previous experience at E.R.) refused to go. The 911 fellows were at a loss, but then decided to call the patient's doctor. After lengthy conversation and a promise by the patient to go to see her doctor the next day, they left shaking their heads. My friend did keep her promise and visited the doctor the next day and several times after that. A diagnosis was never reached.

You're probably wondering how all this came about. Well, I'm sure it was a case of mistaken identity because of a matter of spelling. The main office, way up there in its rather mysterious location, just goofed. You see, my friend has a rather common name. Some people spell the name without an E at the end. She does use the E ending. And then the last name also contains an E. Well, she spells her last name without the E. So I figure it was all a matter of contacting the wrong person. As soon as the spelling errors were rectified, my friend began to feel okay. She's still playing Mah Jong every Wednesday and even winning sometimes.

At the celestial main office, the almighty CEO reviewed the "E" case, as it was now called. His eyes swept over the vast new high tech available. Then he considered the new life-lengthening medical discoveries which were causing a shortage of fresh, experienced recruits. Shaking his mighty head, he concluded, "You just can't get any good help these days."

An American in Barcelona

His parents were out when Roger's call from Barcelona, Spain reached their number in Alabama. Fortunately, his grandmother happened to be visiting. She relayed the troubling message as soon as possible. This message contained a completely new problem for Roger's perplexed parents. Not that they had not been jarred out of their complacency a time or two since Roger had become a Hippie. In fact, this past year or so had added a new dimension to their rather quiet and comfortable lives. They had become accustomed to seeing their son leave for Europe in his torn jeans and unkempt hair and even driving him to the highway where he always seemed to get a ride with some nice person.

The call from Barcelona did come as a complete surprise because the last time they had heard from their "wandering boy" he was on his way to the Canary Islands. They had avoided even thinking of his hitch-hiking across France on the way to Spain.

But back to Barcelona … here's the story. Roger called to tell his family that he was now stranded in Barcelona with only 75 cents in his pocket. He had made arrangements to pick up a certain amount of money (sufficient for his needs) at the American Express Office in Barcelona on his return from the Canary Islands. That plan somehow went awry. There were no funds available for him at American Express. That old axiom about travel being broadening certainly fits this case. That's when Roger learned that some Hippies weren't as honorable and caring as the famous "Flower Children".

Since the president of the local bank was a good friend of Roger's father, he was most willing to help out in this emergency. Even though it was already late in the afternoon, he would contact his bank in New York and see that funds would be wired to Roger at once. These folks weren't aware that the next day was a bank holiday in Spain and therefore, the funds couldn't be delivered until the day after.

When all this became clear to Roger, he began to be very careful with his 75 cents, trying to buy something cheap and nourishing to eat. Luckily he met a fellow Hippie on the street – an American girl easily recognizable by her hippie uniform consisting of torn blue jeans and disheveled hair. She was very kind and gave Roger an apple and 25 cents. Now he was ready to wait out the delay.

The following day Roger waited on a street corner, guitar in hand. He even began to play some music. Maybe someone would toss him a few coins. Instead, he attracted the attention of a poor Spaniard from the surrounding hills. They began to have a conversation. Oh, how Roger now wished he had been a better student in his Spanish class at school. Before he knew exactly what was happening, our boy was invited to go up into the hills to this "amigo's" home. Without hesitation he took up his guitar and climbed up to the peasant's village with his new friend. They soon reached their destination – a small cinder-block house.

In a few hours a crowd gathered around the house. People came from all around the area and some brought their own guitars with them. What a joyful and welcoming group. There was music, laughter, singing and dancing under the stars. They seemed to be very happy with their American guest. A genuine and pleasant rapport soon developed. The festivities lasted until late into the night. These Spanish peasants shared their meager food and wine, their company and their pleasure in the evening. Finally, the festivities came to an end. It was time for everyone to leave for home. The Spaniards bid warm goodbyes to their new-found American friend. "Adiós amigo. Go in peace. Hasta luego, until we meet again."

Roger wound his way back down the hills to the city and to the local Youth Hostel. The next morning at the American Express office all went smoothly and Roger was ready for his departure. “Adiós, Barcelona. Thank you for the kindness of your people and their warm hospitality. Hasta luego.” I’ll no doubt be a lot older by then and maybe a little wiser, thought Roger, but will I be as lucky???

Norman Nood

Norman Nood was really a super salesman. No one could deny it. He sold a large number of sweaters every year. When a merchant noticed Norman entering his establishment, he would try to pull up all his defenses and usually started muttering under his breath, "No. No. No." That didn't do much good because after their encounter and a dose of Nood's persistence and salesmanship, the merchant could only watch the salesman walking out the door with a smile on his face and his book bulging with orders.

Nood was finally forced into mandatory retirement. By then closets all over America were full of "Nood" sweaters. On the first cool day in autumn, people began pulling out these sweaters. Their owners stroked their sweaters fondly and remembered with pleasure these bargains bought the previous season at "over-stocked" sales in clothing and department stores across the land.

In retirement, Norman Nood, who still had plenty of drive and energy, was looking for a positive way to use his talents. He finally decided to do some volunteer work for his country. After all, the U.S. had been very good to him. He made his choice and became chairman of a committee to raise funds to purchase new china for the White House. Within a year, State Dinners there were being served on the new Batheington China made especially for that use. Nood had been completely involved in this undertaking, even helping with the design of the china. The plates were bordered with tiny red, white and blue flags. The centers of the plates pictured the head of a famous past U.S. president and general. During the salad course the serving staff often noticed a startled guest staring into his plate after he'd finished his lettuce while his former leader somberly returned his gaze. Sometimes waiters would notice a trembling hand reach for a water goblet and a comforting sip of water.

The people in charge were becoming accustomed to all this when someone discovered they had received too much Batheington China for the space allowed. About ten place settings had to be "resettled". Nood came to the rescue. He sold off the surplus to wealthy and patriotic citizens as souvenirs and keepsakes. All over the country nice homes and even mansions proudly displayed their pieces of Batheington China.

With that effort done, Norman Nood now looked for new opportunities for serving his fellow countrymen. Why not see that the Batheington China was accompanied by new table silver, procured and designed by Nood himself? On learning about this new project the managers and stewards of the State Dining Rooms turned pale. Shaking their heads, they worried, especially about the design of this new tableware. It was rather late to put any plan into motion now. But for the future they had to think of some means of getting Nood out of their province. Many important people frequented these dining rooms on a regular basis. Perhaps a hint dropped at the right time would do the trick.

On further deliberation a bold plan was conceived. If they were able to get Nood into the right government department he could really do some good. He might have to sell something (maybe California?), but there was no doubt he could get rid of our troubling budget deficit. At any rate, Norman Nood would be out of their dining rooms and all concerned would be so pleased. In a short time, the media were reporting a great improvement in the U.S. GNP, trade balance, and the economy in general. Now the future looked quite promising. Did Norman Nood have anything to do with these changes?? No one heard from Norman. Did he finally feel that he could retire and let some other super-smooth salesman take over?

Until today, no one has heard anything about Nood. He had become a legend in his own time. What a guy! More than that, he has taken his place in the lexicon of a language spoken around the world with varying degrees of fluency. People might not know how this word was derived or understand its origin… but just about everyone with any knowledge of this language recognizes the word in question. It's "Noodnik"!!!

Living & Learning

No one had ever told Hannah that she was beautiful. Her devoted husband had never used those words to her or even blurted them out in their most intimate and loving moments. It didn't matter, really. And it surely was not important in the context of their lives during the disquieting early 1940's. Even so, we know that small things can sometimes tend to make a difference. Our own hang-nails still hurt us.

Early in her marriage Hannah had learned a hard lesson and it stuck. This came about when the young couple went out to buy a new refrigerator. They had an appointment to meet Mr. Jones at his appliance store one evening after work. Their first born was just a few months old and, of course, came along, too - in his mother's arms. After introducing his young wife to Mr. Jones, Hannah was surprised to hear her young husband apologize for his wife's appearance. It was summertime and Hannah wore a cool green and white checked cotton dress. Naturally, she was embarrassed, and hurt, too, by this turn of events. She kept control of her feelings until they arrived back home. And then she began to cry. "Why did you apologize to Mr. Jones about me?" she asked between sobs. "He doesn't mean anything to you. I'm your wife and I know you love and care for me." she continued, feeling miserable. The young husband was aghast. He didn't try to explain or excuse his thoughtlessness, but just held Hannah and tried to comfort her. There was no doubt that he felt terrible about the whole thing and knew that this would never happen again. He had learned a valuable lesson, but so had Hannah.

After that incident Hannah never left her house without first checking her appearance. She was even careful when pushing the baby carriage around the neighborhood or walking down to the A & P grocery store. The young couple reared their children, built their family and matured into responsible members of their community, town and world. Her husband worked hard to support his young family. Hannah never was a compulsive shopper. All that kind of thing was held in what they considered a proper place in their lives.

It came as a bit of a surprise in later years, when she was introduced at a large gathering to the strains of "Pretty Woman!" Oh well, that was probably meant as a tribute to her age and personality. It didn't seem to be condescending at the time. As she grew older and tragedy struck her dearest ones, Hannah learned to cope. Her husband had lost his father on his thirteenth birthday, so from an early age he had developed a sort of protective shell and acceptance of life's changes. Years later, Hannah often thought of the days when her dear husband was hospitalized with a fatal illness. She would always appear neatly dressed. Now she wondered if it was true that she did this to show him her optimism in the face of despair, or was it some foolish form of self absorption? Maybe each person has his own method of trying to live a normal life.

During her later years a strange thing would happen to Hannah, unwilled. Her mind's eye would produce a screen. She didn't have to "log on." It just came from some permanent connection. She would see images of all her loved ones, full of energy and smiles with high spirits. They were beautiful! Only when that view began to fade did age show itself as a force. The picture would lose its lovely brilliance and each person became a pale replica of those so dear to Hannah's heart.

As the "connection" weakened, Hannah always returned to the present. This day Hannah came back with a start. "What time is it?" she wondered. "I have an appointment this afternoon. Gotta get ready to go." She hurried over to her closet to select an outfit for that day. As she moved the hangers on the rod, she looked over her wardrobe. "Navy blue is good with green or red or white. Better make up my mind. It's getting late." Then Hannah stopped and told herself, "This is ridiculous. I'm getting very close to being ninety years old. Who cares how I look? Now where did I put that new white handbag?"

Uncle Yank

"Just say, 'Charge it, Mr. Lipsitz.'" People all around Birmingham (even those who had never set foot in a Credit Store) were repeating, "Just say, 'Charge it, Mr. Lipsitz.'" Newspapers and billboards were displaying this personal message to potential customers who might be interested in buying their clothing on the installment plan.

Everybody was talking and joking about the invitation to "Just say, 'Charge it, Mr. Lipsitz.'" But who was Mr. Lipsitz? If you're really interested, I think I can inform you. I knew a little about him, not everything – just a little. The Lipsitz brothers moved to Birmingham from Savannah, GA. They were just entering manhood. These two young men worked hard and finally owned a business of their own. They were very close to the same age. J.W. Lipsitz was the elder of the two by just a year or two. In personality there was a world of difference. Max, the younger brother, was handsome and outgoing with a very pleasing way about him. No doubt all this was the result of his growing up with a doting mother and four adoring older sisters. After Max married and began to have a family, he and his wife decided to move to another southern city. This brought about the break-up of the brothers' partnership. When this development became public knowledge, the store's suppliers and jobbers of merchandise began to wonder if Lipsitz Credit Store would continue to be a good credit risk. They had been dealing with the charming Max and hardly knew the retiring and quiet J.W. The future proved their worries unfounded. J.W. now took full charge of a thriving business.

Although he did serve in the army during WWII and luckily returned home again unharmed after duty in North Africa and Italy, Yank didn't get his nickname in the war. He had been called Yank long before the War and before moving to Birmingham. As a child, J.W's Jewish name was Yankle (little Jacob). While he was becoming a young man, Yankle got shortened and changed to "Yank" and that name stuck. Yank was just as interesting and unforgettable as his more popular brother, Max. On meeting him you would encounter a rather small man, dapper, well-dressed and always wearing a suit and tie. His voice, deep and resonant, promised some profound utterances and extremely intellectual attitudes. However; after listening to a number of throat clearings and hesitations, you realized that he rarely finished a sentence. His tweeds and ever-present pipe still pictured – at least – an Oxford Don.

Yank did love good books and good music. The grand piano in the family living room was beginning to bend under the weight of all his L.P records. In the past that piano had been the source of some pleasure. One of the nephews played it quite well. Also because of that instrument, Yank's life was brightened for a time. There might have been some thoughts of a happy future in the offing. Here's how that came about. Yank's mother had offered the use of their piano to a young girl pianist for almost daily practicing sessions. Her family had come on hard times and moved to Birmingham sans a piano of its own. This young musician appealed to Yank. She was fresh and cultured with a delightful musical talent. Yank often came home early to be present and listen to her play. He sometimes escorted her safely home. It isn't known whether or not anything more serious could have come of this. After all, Yank was much older and she young and inexperienced. Did either of them ever make a tiny step toward becoming more intimate? Probably not – but who knows?

Losing his mother was a very sad blow for Yank. After her death, he remained in the family home, for a time with one of his sisters. Over the years Yank had been really generous and attentive to his sisters and their children. Yet, he appeared to be a very lonely man and rather mysterious as far as his inner life and feelings were concerned. Once we heard something about his relations with another young woman. Why that didn't develop is anyone's guess. Yank's long time and devoted driver, Little Richard, surely knew him best. Some members of the family may have questioned Little Richard, but they are all gone now.

How did Yank's story end? The truth is that he decided to end it himself – in his neglected home – with a revolver – leaving no note of explanation. So he remains an enigma. Still, Yank lives on in the memories of the people who knew him as well as he could allow anyone to get to really know him.

An Empty Place

Anya knew she'd had a really good and blessed life. But whenever the subject of formal education came up, there was an empty feeling in her breast - maybe somewhere around the heart – a feeling almost like embarrassment.

As the youngest of four children of rather cultured and genteel immigrant parents, she had been cherished, loved and even "babied." But the rule was that everyone must "pitch in" and help as soon as high school was completed. It was really a pleasant household. Friends were always welcome. Mama was well-read and serious, even severe at times, but with a surprising sense of humor. Papa was hard working, kind and compassionate, but he had never managed to "come back" after the great depression when he lost everything, even the family home. At sixteen, upon graduation from high school, there was nothing for Anya to do but go to work. There were plenty of people in the same circumstances. Those were hard times for most of the young people in Anya's crowd and life went on with hope for a better future. Anya married young to her childhood sweetheart. They were happy together, reared three lovely children and took each day as it came. Life was good despite the tribulations that came along without invitation. Illness and loss were overshadowed by business success, finding one's place and contributing to society in general.

Still, that empty space persisted in spite of classes at the local college, art and voice lessons, extensive travel and even exploring many books assigned to her children. One year, Anya devoted much time to discovering William Faulkner. While reading *My Brother Bill* by John Faulkner, Anya found a delightful friend. John was apparently such an easy person to know. He was understanding and open, with a keen sense of humor. Anya decided to write and thank him for his lovely book. (She probably could not have considered writing to the "great man" himself.)

A few weeks later, a letter arrived from Oxford, Mississippi. It was written in a spidery, artistic handwriting and was from John Faulkner's widow. She explained that her husband had recently died, but she knew he would have very much appreciated Anya's letter and would have certainly responded had he been able. So this letter was being written for him. Anya realized that letter was something very special in her life and carefully put it away in her copy of *My Brother Bill*.

Some years later, and after many changes for Anya, she found herself alone in her house. Always looking forward, she agreed to join some friends in attending an Elderhostel at the University of Mississippi in Oxford. One of the subjects was intriguing: “The Southern Mystique”. Remembering her letter from Oxford, she decided to take it along. Someone there might be interested.

Upon arriving at the University, Anya showed the letter to the beautiful young woman in charge of her group and asked if she thought it might be of interest to anyone. The young woman took the letter with her. The next morning she approached Anya and told her, “You are now in the Faulkner Archives. The University will write you a letter of acknowledgement soon.” And they did.

What a surprise and what a thrill! The empty place in Anya's breast was filled with wonder. Her name was now a part of history, even though minute. Still, to be in such important and respected company!

But then Anya thought most people, even illustrious ones, probably aren't that different from you and me. A person doesn't have to be very talented or born to wealth and position to reap life's pleasures. The most wonderful things can happen to anyone.

Looking Within

Everybody went on about their business as though it was a normal day. Nothing special! And like most people my friend Eve felt the same way. As for the time and place; it involved just a few hours. And the place wasn't that glamorous either. Eve had spent most of her life there and had chosen to grow old in familiar surroundings and among dear and cherished friends and family. As for family, most close relatives were long gone though still very much present in memory. The younger generations kept life interesting with their vivacity, their unbridled zest and sometimes their cock-eyed perception. What their world will be like is anybody's guess.

As you can see, this isn't a deep study of life. It's about a few hours spent reflecting on the life of my good, lifelong friend Eve; certainly, it didn't affect general world conditions or large populations one way or the other. Still, with these hours, deep feeling and pleasure in one precious life surfaced.

What happened? Did some long lost friend show up? Was it a romantic interlude at this late date? Was some lost treasure found and retrieved? It wasn't any of these. Nevertheless, there was discovery of a kind – self discovery which brought Eve a new perspective on herself as a person.

She finally came to realize her fragile self-worth. With that inward exploration, Eve came upon a great treasure indeed. She now viewed a life lived, not perfectly, but pretty much up to her abilities, a life in which she would probably go on making mistakes in spite of her best efforts. Still, during these special hours Eve had finally accepted a really marvelous gift. She examined her gift with wonder and was able to give it a name – contentment. What a blessing! Well, it wasn't long before Eve heard a familiar, taunting, inner-voice speak to her, "Come on. Do you really think this is gonna last?"

Acknowledgements

This memoir owes so much to so many people that I am hesitant in mentioning specific names. However, on reflection I feel that I owe everything to my dear and loving family for giving me a life history that I cherish and remember with great wonder and pleasure. Surely they have fostered in me a desire to pass on my memories to their descendents and mine. For all that I am indeed grateful.

To my children Eileen and Robert Cohn I owe much for their patient perusal of this work in progress and their encouragement to continue over many years. Without Eileen and Howard Sarasohn, I probably would not have had the will to continue writing. A published author of talent and experience, Eileen's approval and suggestions gave me the courage to go on. To my granddaughter, Abbey, I owe much appreciation for the time she spent typing and sharing her computer skills to my great advantage. My "number one editor" grandson Jacob Speaks has my deepest gratitude for the many hours he has devoted to organizing this manuscript. His patience and understanding have been my support throughout these past months. Our telephone conversations have not only brought about improvement of the text, but have engendered personal calm and contentment. Jacob's expertise is certainly evident in the finished offering. There aren't enough words at my disposal to acknowledge all the hours my dear friend Rachel Polhill (a retired college librarian) has contributed by reading and co-editing this memoir. Her knowledge has been invaluable. Also, Rachel's willingness and experience has greatly eased my anxiety on actual decisions to be made with the book publisher. Besides all this, her company is a source of real pleasure. Each of these lovely people has my never-ending thanks.